Shannon Woodward is the wise and witty friend from whom you can always borrow a cup of grace. Like new-fallen snow on the tongue, her honest insights refresh the restless soul. Whatever season you're in, let A *Whisper in Winter* help you make sense of it.

—Clint Kelly,
author of *Dare to Raise Exceptional Children*

A *Whisper in Winter* offers readers glory on every page. But how could it not, for each chapter is a fireside chat with wisdom. To be sure, Shannon's extraordinary insights into the ordinary seasons of life will cause her readers to ask themselves, "If God has been whispering to me, why haven't I been listening?"

—James Hansen,
pastor of Antioch Bible Church and
academic dean of Imago Dei Institute

A Whisper in Winter

Ruth,

I thoroughly enjoyed spending this weekend with you & the ladies of CC South Hill. May God bless you abundantly!

Shannon
Is. 30:21

A Whisper in Winter

Stories of Hearing God's Voice
in Every Season of Life

SHANNON WOODWARD

new
hope
PUBLISHERS

Birmingham, Alabama

New Hope® Publishers
P. O. Box 12065
Birmingham, AL 35202-2065
www.newhopepublishers.com

Library of Congress Cataloging-in-Publication Data
Woodward, Shannon.
A whisper in winter : stories of hearing God's voice in every season of life / by Shannon Woodward.
p. cm.
ISBN 1-56309-823-7 (pbk.)
1.   Christian life-Meditations. I. Title.
BV4501.3.W66 2004
148—dc22
2004015658

ISBN: 1-56309-823-7

N044111 • 1004 • 4.5M1

Dedicated with much gratitude to:

Dave, Zac, and Tera Woodward—for loving me through the tough seasons, laughing with me in the good, and teaching me to hear God's whispers

and

Our church family at Calvary Chapel of Marysville, Washington—for opening their hearts, sharing their stories, and making it such a joy to be a pastor's wife.

Table of Contents

Acknowledgments

I'd like to thank Joan Biggar Husby, Kimn Gollnick, and Christopher and Cora Welch for reading my rough drafts and making suggestions. You'll never know how much I needed your fresh eyes and your kindness.

I owe many thanks to the team at New Hope—my editor, Rebecca England, Lynn Waldrep, Tara Miller, Tamzen Benfield, and all the rest who helped me through this process. Thanks go also to Jon Walker, who has mentored my writing for years, and to Becky Yates, who saw a germ of an idea in something I said and helped shape the direction of this book. I should also thank Diana Green, who sat across from me in a restaurant one night and, upon learning that I wrote, asked, "So if you're a writer, how come you're not writing a book?" Nudges help.

And, always . . . thank You, Father, for choosing me, wooing me, and making me Your own. Your voice means everything to me—and I cannot wait for the day when I put a face to the sound I love so much.

Please visit me at www.shannonwoodward.com

Introduction

I sat at my desk and tried hard to concentrate on the words on the computer screen, but scenes of my day with my four-year-old son kept flashing through my mind, interrupting my thoughts. Zac crying…arguing…stomping to his room. Finally I gave up and rested my forehead in my hands. How had this day gone so wrong?

After four years of motherhood, I expected more from myself. By this time, I figured, I should be pretty competent. But nothing in my bag of tricks had made the slightest dent in my son's determination that day. If I said "Go left," he went right. If I said "Sit up," he scooted down as far as possible. Black was white and yes was no. A whole day of sparring and correcting had left me exhausted, frustrated, and glum.

I'd tried gentle. I'd tried firm. He'd been sent to "time out" so many times that I was certain, if I checked, the bench seat would still be warm. By bedtime we had reached an uneasy truce. We'd hugged, shared a story, and prayed together. Still, my sense of failure lingered.

As I stared at my keyboard and replayed each of the day's failures, I heard a tiny shuffling coming down the hall—the sound of little slippers swishing across carpet. One green eye, and then the other, peeked around the doorjamb.

"You're up," I observed.

He nodded.

"Is something wrong?"

"Kinda."

Maybe he shared my uneasiness about the day. Maybe

he, too, felt there was a little unfinished business between us. He kicked an imaginary spot on the carpet. He scratched another invisible spot on the wall, then rubbed his nose.

Finally, he gave a little sigh. "I was just wondering something. Mom, will you ever…will you ever unlove me?"

Oh, honey.

I couldn't get out of my chair fast enough. I scooped him up and squeezed his little flanneled body and rocked—as if rocking could shake out all his doubts.

"Don't you know that nothing could ever, ever, ever make me unlove you?"

"Even ten bad days?"

"Even ten hundred."

He twirled a strand of my hair between his fingers. "I just wanted to know."

I heard God whisper that night. He arranged that little conversation to unstop the ears of my heart, and then He whispered:

I'll never unlove you.

He knows I wonder now and then. Because now and then I let Him down. I fail to be the wife, the mother, the daughter, the friend I know I should be. At those times, my failures loom large enough to block out the sight of His loving face. I question His commitment, sure that I've finally reached the end of His patience.

I forget that I am, after all, only a child. I forget that He is a parent with unending love.

All I really need is a quiet reminder. And so He whispers, with a voice so tender and compassionate that the sound alone melts my insecurities and rights my soul.

I think you need those whispers, too. Because I think you're just like me. You're a woman juggling ten different roles and not always juggling successfully. Oh, there are days when the right words come out of your mouth and the right choices seem effortless, but then there are those other days—days when you wander off the path and say all the wrong things and end up hurting the ones you love. Days when every step is a move backwards, and by bedtime you've gone a dozen miles in the wrong direction.

God wants to reassure us that no matter how far we slip, no matter how far we wander, nothing will ever make Him unlove us. He whispers that and a hundred equally astonishing truths every day, but if we don't slow down long enough to take a second listen, we miss it. The noise of life drowns out the passion of His voice.

I wrote this book to tell you one thing: your God loves you. Not just a little—but a lot. Deeply. Want to know how much? So much that since your first tiny lungful, He's taken note of every breath you've ever drawn. He's measured out all your heartbeats. The sound of your crying moves Him so much He saves every tear you shed. He loves to hear you laugh, and when you triumph in some small way, He applauds your victory. Though you may think differently, the truth is that God is on your side—and He loves you fervently. He's not disappointed in you. He's not angry that you haven't achieved perfection. He doesn't scowl when you drop one of the ten plates you've been spinning. Instead, He leans close and whispers, "I'll never unlove you."

The stories you'll find here are not profound. In fact, the moments I've written about are all quite ordinary. But that should be an encouragement to those of us living ordinary lives. Take heart: God does not speak solely through burning bushes. He speaks through the murmurings of an infant, the laughter of an old woman, the questions of a four-year-old. Listen, and you'll hear His gentle whisper. It's speaking your name.

Is this book for you? It is if you've ever felt invisible…insignificant…alone…defeated…anxious…restless…overwhelmed.

It's for you if this is a time of spiritual spring—you're in a moment of renewal or at the start of a brand new chapter in life. It may be that you've just been forgiven. The slate was wiped clean and God gave you a little pat and a smile and sent you back out to play. Or maybe you've just recently been adopted into His family. Everything is fresh, new, inviting. God's whispers are there to help you on your feet: "Take My hand."

Perhaps it's a season of summer for you. The clouds parted, and you caught a glimpse of the truth. You got it. You figured out—finally—that it's not about striving and doing. It's simply about enjoying Him. You don't have to work to please your Father, you just have to keep holding His hand and see where He takes you. God is there to whisper, "Let's walk."

It could be that you're in spiritual autumn. For some reason, you've begun to shoulder the load again. Though you know, deep down, that all things come from and through His hand, you've let yourself slip into an anxious mood. You feel that everything is up to you, and if you're to be protected and provided for, you have to do it for yourself. God is there to whisper, "Not so."

For you women in a season of winter, my heart is with you. I'm in winter too, right now. As I write this book, I'm still grieving a few losses of my own. In this season of barrenness, when everything seems lifeless and spring looks years away, let God breathe the comfort your soul aches for. Let Him remind you, "I'm here."

This book is a gentle model. Whether you absorb them in one sitting or a dozen, randomly or in order, the stories within will teach the art of listening. I'll tell you the whispers I've heard, and then you start listening for your own. They'll be there. They've been there all along.

My hope is that these stories will take you by the hand and walk you closer toward the heart of God. His greatest desire is to be known by you. From the majestic to the mundane, His voice calls out. In the pounding of the ocean's surf, in the clap and flash of lightning, He roars.

In the midst of ordinary moments, He whispers.

Summer

"A time to laugh…a time to dance"

I've given this a lot of thought, and I've come to the conclusion that God gave me children so I would understand Him better. Nothing else has opened my eyes to His love more than the experience of loving my children.

The most amazing moment for me, as a parent, was that first moment. Unlike most other mothers, I didn't get my first glimpse of my son when he was all slippery and irritated. Because we were adoptive parents, we had to wait for a phone call inviting us to the hospital. Zac was an hour old by the time Dave and I got there, and by then he was all cleaned up and calmed down. When the nurse placed him in my arms and I said "Hello" to that little face, he opened his eyes and looked directly into mine. It was as if I could read his thoughts, as if I could actually hear him thinking, "Oh…there you are." I just stood there and cried.

I didn't know it was possible to love another person as much as I loved him in that first moment. When I felt those eight pounds, one ounce lying helpless in my arms, my heart was full to bursting with feelings of protection and delight and pure satisfaction. There wasn't a single second when I thought, "Well, little guy, I guess I'll accept you the way you are right now, because I have no other choice…but I'm *really* going to start loving you when you can walk." Or, "I'll love you best when you've figured me out—when you know that my favorite colors are blue and green and the ice

21

cream I like best is peanut butter chocolate. When you know that I light candles at the first sign of rain. When you've memorized all those little details, then I'll *really* start loving you."

I didn't think any of that nonsense. I don't believe Zac had any such strange thoughts, either. I'm pretty sure there wasn't even a second there, at the hospital, when he worried that he might not be a good son or that he might not work hard enough or manage to create anything worthy in his lifetime. I don't think it ever crossed his little mind that he might not measure up to my expectations. Nor did he worry about where we had the car parked, or whether or not we had enough gas, or if Dave really knew how to maneuver us from the hospital back to the freeway and all the way home. He just looked up at the two of us and waited to see what was next. And you know what was next? A lot of staring and grinning. A lot of dreaming about the life we would have with him. And a whole lot of loving.

God is no different. He feels exactly the same way—He loves us just the way we love our children, only He does it much better. I hope you really grab hold of the truth behind these words: Your Father is not waiting to love you more, because He already loves you as much as He possibly can. He loves you perfectly, flawlessly. It's not because of anything you can do for Him. It's not because you try really hard to walk a straight line. It's not because you're diligent to read your Bible exactly thirty minutes each morning, followed by a precise fifteen minutes of prayer. He just…loves you. And the child who understands this is the child who is free—free to explore life and enjoy her Father and face tomorrow without fear of any kind.

The stories in this section all illustrate the summers of a believer's life: those moments when she realizes there's nothing she can do to make God more delighted with her than He already is. Summer is a time of pure joy and unhindered freedom. It is a time to run with abandon. When you grasp how completely and eternally you are loved by God, you stop worrying about everything else, because nothing else matters anymore. All that's left is the relationship He offers.

I hope you experience endless summer. It's the place to be. Ideally, we would all live there, all the time—in a constant state of blissful freedom.

My prayer is that as you read through these stories, you'll begin to rest in God's perfect love, and maybe for the first time in a long time, you'll stop struggling and striving. Open your eyes and look up, and you'll see an amazing sight: God is looking right back at you. He can't help it. Your Father loves you so much, He can't take His eyes off you.

1

The Swinging Bridge

"But the people who know their God shall be strong and do great things."

—Daniel 11:32 (TLB)

The bridge had been there all along, living somewhere in my memory—tucked away with other relics from childhood in a deep, quiet corner. I rarely ever thought of it, except once in a great while when the sound of rushing water or splashing feet would carry my thoughts back to this very spot. I stood on top of the steep dirt bank and stared down at the bridge for the first time in twenty years. It looked different, I decided. Or maybe all the changes had occurred in me.

Zac, then five, let go of my hand and started down the embankment. His younger cousin, Christian, followed.

"I'll betcha I can get down there first," Zac said.

I watched the boys scrambling to beat each other, and twenty years melted away. I remembered those summer days when I was the one issuing all the challenges.

"Beatcha to the bridge!" I'd shout. Before my mother could bring her little red Corvair to a complete stop, my two sisters and I would fling open our doors and dash out. We'd rush down the hill, dragging our beach towels behind us in the dirt and taunting one another.

At the bottom of the embankment thirty feet of sand separated us from our goal. The bridge hung there like a giant looming mystery. "Come and conquer me," it seemed to invite. We'd toss our towels, sprint across the sun-heated ground, and lunge onto the wooden structure. Mid-leap, like clockwork, I'd hear my mother's voice drift down from high on the hill. "Hold the railing!" she called out, every single time. I never understood why she kept saying that. More than likely, it was pure habit. She said it, knowing she was supposed to. Knowing also that we wouldn't listen. We didn't see the need. Having crossed its girth dozens of times, we trusted the old bridge. We'd all but memorized the number of planks that carried our steps over the expanse of river. In our childish wisdom, we knew it was safe.

I didn't know what had brought me back to the bridge after so many years. I'd set out that morning with a short list of errands, none of which involved or included a trip to my childhood. In my purse was a large manila envelope containing my husband's application to a seminary in Portland, Oregon. Getting that envelope in the mail was my most important task of the day. After that, I had planned to take the boys to the park. But driving downtown to the Marysville post office, I had felt a nudge to alter my plans. Before I really understood what I was doing, my car was headed toward Granite Falls and making a left turn on the Jordan Road.

And there it was, right in front of me—the bridge of my long-ago summer days. I stared at the structure and entertained an odd thought. It would be quite easy to walk out to the center of the bridge and drop that manila envelope right over the side.

I shook off the guilty thought and started down the hill. It wasn't anywhere near as effortless as I remembered. Zac and Christian had no trouble at all navigating the bank, but somehow I had left my grace—and my center of gravity— back in my childhood. I slid and slipped my way all the way down the slope. Near the bottom, I risked a glance away from my feet just long enough to see the boys approaching the edge of the bridge.

"Wait for me!" I yelled.

They waited. Not because I'd asked them to. Not out of politeness. They waited simply because they hadn't yet mustered enough courage to step forward.

I walked up behind them and stopped. The bridge had indeed changed. Metal meshing had replaced the old wooden planks. Where simple cables had once sufficed, elaborate wires and cross beams now supported the contraption. Chin-high metal railings now guarded both sides, but back then the sides were easily climbed by the throngs of teenagers who used to dive from its edge into the river below.

Progress had changed the old bridge, but it hadn't quite managed to remove the awe factor.

"I'm scared," Christian stated, digging his heels in the sand at the bridge's edge.

Zac nodded. "I'm scared it's gonna break and we'll fall in the river."

"Nope," I said. "It won't break. If there was even a chance of that, I'd never let you on it."

I offered them each a hand. Christian's grip was vise like, but Zac quickly acclimated himself to the bridge's gentle swaying and let go of my hand. He took a few steps, broke into a wide smile, and started running.

When he reached the center of the span, he stopped and stared at the view below his feet. "Hey, Christian! Look down—you can see the river!"

Christian wasn't impressed with the sight of all that water just beneath the thin-looking mesh. He tightened his grip again, momentarily, but within a few minutes curiosity got the better of him. Soon he was down on his knees, peering at the river.

"It's far down," he observed.

Then he stood, took a few tentative steps toward Zac, and began running.

I leaned over the railing and looked at the ripples below, and felt that odd impulse again. Just toss the envelope into the river and be done with it.

For a second time, the thought shamed me. My husband, I knew, was going to be an incredible pastor. He loved the Lord like no one I had ever met, and his heart was that of a shepherd. It wasn't Dave I was worried about. It was me. If he was going to be a pastor, then by default that made me a pastor's wife. And I just couldn't see it.

My mind revisited each of the pastor's wives I'd known. Rhonda had been quiet and calm. Heather was an amazing piano player. Teresa had it all—beauty, grace, and wisdom. I simply couldn't imagine joining this group of women.

What if I couldn't be who everyone needed me to be? What if—in me—there wasn't enough wise old owl to satisfy people's expectations? What if I couldn't find Bible verses when people asked for them? What if I didn't have anything profound to say when the phone rang?

The idea of failing terrified me, and the list of ways I might disappoint people seemed endless. I knew I laughed too much, or maybe just too boisterously. I just couldn't help it. For the most part, life seemed pretty funny to me. But none of the pastors' wives I knew were like that.

Then there were silly things, like movies. I went once in a while—to appropriate movies only, but still, what if someone disapproved? I liked Disneyland—a lot. At the time, liking Disneyland wasn't acceptable in a lot of church circles. I didn't have a pastor's wife's wardrobe. I nearly lived in my jeans, and I didn't see that changing anytime soon. What would people think when they ran into me at the grocery store?

It just went on and on.

I stood there for a bit, mulling over still more of my short-comings, when God began dealing with me.

Look at the boys.

I looked.

What do you see?

The two were at the far end of the span, jumping up and down. Zac was utilizing every bit of five-year old leg muscle to try to get the biggest ride possible out of the bridge. Christian was laughing so hard he could barely catch his breath.

Where is their fear?

I didn't know where it went. It was just gone.

Had I been afraid the first time I came to the bridge? I couldn't recall. But I did remember the reactions of others. The bridge was a local attraction, the sort of place people brought their visiting relatives to see. As a young girl, I thought it funny to watch newcomers as they made their way down the dirt hill.

"My word! Is that thing safe?" some would ask. This, while watching us kids prancing up and down the trembling structure. Our combined weight was slight back then, but it was still enough to make for a wild ride on the bridge.

"You're not getting me on that contraption," others would declare. I recall watching those cautious few settle themselves on the safety of the bank, where they'd watch the goings-on and occasionally shake their head at our reck-lessness.

"You're missing out," I'd always think. I felt pity for them. I wouldn't have traded the freedom I felt out there, sus-pended over the swirling Stillaguamish River, for anything.

No, I couldn't remember ever being afraid of the bridge. But there must have been a moment, like there was with Zac and Christian, when I felt trepidation. I supposed it went away after a few tentative hops. Like the boys, once I'd tested the bridge and found it to be trustworthy, my fear probably vanished.

But you're afraid now.

"Yes, Lord, but of much bigger things."

Look again at the boys.

So He was trying to show me something. I looked again, and tried to understand what I was seeing.

The boys started out afraid, and now they were fearless. In just a few short minutes, their fear had been replaced with freedom, their apprehension with boldness. As far as I could tell, they hadn't done much to cause this transformation. They'd simply taken a first step. They'd run their hands along the railing and jumped up and down and tested the mesh beneath their feet and found it all to be trustworthy.

Have you tested Me?

What did He mean?

Am I trustworthy?

Of course He was trustworthy. I knew He was. I thought of all the times I'd needed my Father, and how He appeared every time to calm my anxieties and supply my needs and hold my hand.

I thought about the recent plane trip I'd taken to see my sister-in-law in Louisiana. A group of family members had gone together, but because I had to come home early, I made the return trip alone. I was full of apprehension, not only because the plane had two stops to make on the way to Seattle but also because that very week the airline I was flying with had a horrific airplane crash. My departure was at 5:30 A.M., and as the plane took off I watched a lightning storm fragmenting the pre-dawn sky in the distance. I was certain I'd be on the evening news.

My Bible was in my carry-on bag. Flipping on the overhead light I began scanning the Psalms. Not a minute into my perusal I came upon these words in Psalm 46:

"God is our refuge and strength,
an ever-present help in trouble.
Therefore we will not fear, though the earth give way
and the mountains fall into the heart of the sea,
though its waters roar and foam
and the mountain quake with their surging."

I read this passage over and over until its truth erased the fear I had been harboring. My God created the very air upon which the airplane was flying. He held me in the palm of His hand, and no matter what happened, He was in control.

I remembered other moments when I'd been afraid, or overwhelmed, or curled up in the clutches of grief. I remembered that my God had been there with me, every single time.

"Yes, Lord, I've tested You."

And what have you learned?

"That You never fail me, Father. Never."

He opened my eyes as I stood there, and I saw that my faith was like the swinging bridge. It seemed to hang on nothing, but even when the winds whipped and shook the cables, even when the river rose and sloshed against its sides, the bridge held firm.

I looked behind me at the bank and thought of all the people hunkered down there. People who were afraid to trust their faith. People who didn't understand what it was to run across the bridge with joyful unrestraint.

I didn't want to be one of those fearful ones. I didn't want to miss out. I knew the choice was there. If I really wanted to, I could pull back. I could run to the safety of the bank and perch there, watching life happen all around me.

But that wasn't what I wanted. I wanted the freedom of "yee-hawing" at the sky while the river raged beneath my feet.

Do you trust Me? He asked again.

"I do, Father. I trust You."

Then run with abandon. I won't let you fall.

I stood and faced the sky. My heart felt full of hope and expectation. Good things were coming. He wouldn't let me fail. I gave the river one final look, and tucked the sound of its lapping waves in that far corner of my memory.

"Hey, boys! Want to get a milkshake?"

They answered with an exuberant "yes" and galloped toward me.

If memory served me right, Ike's Restaurant in downtown Granite Falls had amazing milkshakes...and it was only a few short blocks from the post office.

2

How precious it is, Lord, to realize that you are thinking about me constantly! I can't even count how many times a day your thoughts turn towards me. And when I waken in the morning, you are still thinking of me!

—Psalm 139:17 (TLB)

"Let's go, let's go, *let's* GO!"

I sink further into my folding chair as the echoes assault my ears. I've only been in the school gym five minutes and already I'm claustrophobic. How does that happen in a room with a forty-foot ceiling?

Please, Coach, I beg silently, *please don't yell at my boy.*

"Zachary—we're not here to skip around the gym. Grab a ball!"

He's yelling.

I begin my silent pleading again, but this time I bypass the coach and go over his head. Way over his head.

Oh, Lord—I can't do this. I can't sit here and watch the coach watch Zac who's not watching anything but that one crazy, flickering ceiling light. I can't sit here and wait for him to get in trouble. Please stop this. Make the coach be nice.

Something—maybe the Lord?—urges me to pick up my book and ignore the scene on the court.

I read twelve words, and then I hear his name again.

"Zachary! Hey, Zachary—what position are you today? You're a forward, *a forward*! That means you have to guard Alex. Do you want him to make a basket and have it be your fault?"

It's a rhetorical question, and not even directed at me, but I answer anyway. *Of course not, Coach. I don't want that.* I hope, briefly, that he hears my unspoken answer-by-proxy and lightens up. I know the truth, though. Zac wouldn't mind a bit if Alex got a basket. He happens to like Alex, and this happens to just be a practice game, for crying out loud.

The coach has words, warnings, and lectures for the other boys too, but somehow I'm able to read my book past those echoes with no more than the slightest register. Every time I hear his lips forming a "z" sound, though, my eyes lock on his face. Time drops to its knees and crawls while I wait for the rest of the coach's word, although there's no question, really, about who he's berating. There are no Zanes, Zekes, or Zeds out there. Only my Zac.

Only Zac, for whom the gym floor is nothing more than an indoor skipping-hopping-galloping surface. Zac, for whom the painted black arcs and lines are imaginary tightropes. Zac, who tries every week to jump higher so he can see out the impossibly high windows. "Maybe I grew this week, Mom. You never know."

He revels in things sensory. When the coach calls them all to the center of the floor for a midget huddle, Zac tries hard to concentrate. He makes a fairly good showing, but I know—because I'm his mother and mothers know everything—that he's really thinking about how to get the loudest and longest squeal out of his tennis shoes the next time he charges down court. I know he's counting the kids and wondering if he should invite them all to his birthday party, even though it's four months away. He's noticing the dampness under his arms and formulating a really good argument for buying deodorant, one he'll try on me the moment practice is over. "Mom, when I get hot, my armpits get all yucky and horrible. It's time, Mom. I am eight now, you know."

The huddle ends. Zac collects his thoughts and makes an adult, "I-mean-business-this-time" kind of face. At least a portion of the coach's lecture permeated Zac's brain. I can see within the first ten seconds that he's made up his mind to be the world's best guard. Poor Joey. He doesn't stand a chance. As the white shirts take the ball down court, Joey discovers he's grown a second skin. He moves left. Zac moves left. He breathes. Zac breathes. He blinks, he spins, he runs. Zac follows every move, the perfect shadow, the perfect little mime. I feel the first sense of relief I've felt since entering the gym. Surely the coach will notice his doggedness and praise him for such tenacity.

The blue shirts get the rebound and head to my end of the court. Zac is still shadowing Joey. As little as I know about basketball, I know enough that I'm pretty sure it's Joey's turn to guard Zac. I'm all but certain Zac is supposed to be trying to get away from Joey now. But no. He follows Joey into a corner and continues his mirroring.

"Zac!" I whisper as loudly as I dare.

He's too busy guarding his own guard to notice.

I clear my throat and try a slightly more intense version of the first whisper. "Zachary!"

I notice with my peripheral vision that the father next to me has glanced over to see what is so urgent. *Ignore me*, I demand wordlessly. *I'm just a crazy, overprotective mother trying to spare her son a little misery. That's it...go back to your sports page...*

"Zac!"

This time it isn't me. It's the coach. He's noticed Zac's tenacity, all right—but on the wrong side of the court.

"Why on earth are you doing that? You're supposed to be getting *away* from Joey! Look at Peter there. He's open. He's standing there waving his arms and making it easy for someone to pass him the ball. That's what you should be doing."

Zac nods his little "yes, sir" nod. Invisible hands strap me to my seat, preventing me from marching out and giving the coach a piece of my mind. At this point it would be the last piece.

The coach blows his whistle. "You guys need to take this more seriously. This is serious business. No goofing off. This game counts! It COUNTS!"

Again with the intensity. What is he talking about? It's practice! I glance down the meager row of parents lining the court. I don't see any scouts. Even if there were—even if a whole bunch of scouts had snuck in, noticed Zac's prowess, and started a bidding war over him—I'd really have to insist that he finish third grade before signing any deals.

Zac gets the ball. He dribbles, stops, dribbles again, and shoots. It's short.

"Short!" the coach yells.

"We know!" I growl.

Sports page dad glances over. I consider asking him what the point of all this is. Am I supposed to just hand my son over to this...this...professional man-maker and let him work his magical wonders? Is that it? Is this some sort of rite of passage intended to turn my humming, skipping, ball-sharing boy into a serious competitor? And if so, why? So that someday he can become a sports page-reading father himself?

Before I can begin my tirade, Zac gets the ball again. I hold my breath as he dribbles. He dodges Joey. He spins around Alex. He lifts the ball and shoots. All eyes follow the arc of the ball as it approaches the net and swooshes through.

A couple of parents clap. The coach yells again, but this time he's cheering, "Great shot, Zac!" He jogs over and slaps his hand. Zac grins. He'll carry that high five all week.

Me? I've been proud of him all along.

I talk to the Lord again. This time I'm not begging for intervention; this time I just need my Father. I tell Him how frustrated I am, how I *don't* understand how the coach *won't* understand that Zac *can't* understand what the big deal is.

I tell Him it's not a love of basketball that keeps my little boy getting up early on Saturday mornings—it's simply a love of being eight. It's the exhilaration of grabbing that beautiful bumpy ball and feeling the cool-but-stale gym air caress his face as he charges down the miles-long floor. It's the chance to lounge against the back wall with two or three of his teammates, laughing together in fake tiredness while they fan their shirts and talk about the candy they have at home stashed in their p.j. drawers. It's all that. Nothing more.

God listens. And then He whispers.

He tells me He understands. He shows me, in a vast and indescribable moment of revelation, my own court in a game called Life. He points out His position, there on the side of the court, where His eyes never leave me and His heart beats in sync with mine.

He tells me how proud He is of me when I resist the pressure to become point-minded. He tells me He loves it when I share the ball, when I don't mind someone else taking it down court, when I cheer for a teammate who finally gets enough coordination to dribble.

And He tells me to never stop. He tells me this game was made for His pleasure, and as far as He's concerned, I can hop all the way down court if I want to.

He tells me I've already won.

"Mom? Mom!"

There he is. My sweaty little game boy, with flushed cheeks and one pink ear, a sure sign to me, his eagle-eyed mother, that he's played hard.

"What, honey?"

"I have this problem. When I'm out there running and I get hot, my armpits get all buttery and slickerish. It's really horrible."

"Hmmm. I guess we know what that means," I say.

"Are you telling me…are you saying…?"

"Yep. We'd better stop by the store on the way home. After all, you are eight now."

He hops all the way to the car.

3

Whispers

"And he has committed to us the message of reconciliation. We are therefore Christ's ambassadors, as though God were making his appeal through us."

—2 Corinthians 5:19–20

Take Tiffany with you.

There was that horrible thought again. I couldn't shake it.

Take Tiffany with you.

It was a miserable drip of a thought—a nagging, annoying, constant interruption. I tried to squelch it by running through my list again. Sunscreen, camera, juice....

Take Tiffany with you.

I stopped packing long enough to argue. Why on earth would I want to invite that child on a day trip to Mt. St. Helens?

Of all the children living in our apartment complex, Tiffany was the last one I'd dream of spending the day with.

As I continued packing, I thought back over the months since we'd moved from our small, secluded farm to this noisy apartment building. When Dave first suggested the move, I agreed instantly. He'd be closer to his seminary and wouldn't have to take the train to commute down to his classes. We could get involved in activities on campus. On top of that, I was excited about the idea of having neighbors for a change. What fun, I thought, to just walk ten steps and knock on someone's door. "Hello," I pictured myself saying. "Can I borrow a cup of sugar? And, hey—as long as I'm here, what do you say we start a Bible study together?"

Reality seldom matches fantasy. It didn't exactly work out the way I'd hoped. None of the women I met at the mailbox cared to meet again. Those I tried to talk to in the apartment clubhouse weren't interested in chatting. I gave up on the sugar-borrowing, but I couldn't give up my vision of starting a women's Bible study.

"Lord," I'd whine occasionally. "I just know I'm supposed to be ministering to these women. When will You open a door?"

More than once, I sensed the same answer: *Trust Me.*

The women weren't responding to my efforts, but their children were another matter. I'm not an exceptional parent. But our front door was always open, there was usually something cooking or just coming out of the oven, and we used strange implements at dinner that drew gossipy comments from the neighbor kids.

"I seen 'em lighting candles last night. The 'lectricity wasn't even off."

"Robby said they don't throw their napkins away. She washes 'em."

"They all sit at the table. And no TV. What's up with that?"

They'd loiter near our door around dinnertime and accost Zac when he headed outside. "What'd ya eat?"

I couldn't understand their curiosity until one evening when I happened to walk past a neighbor's open door. Inside the darkened room I saw Tiffany, whom we'd recently met, standing near the television. She held a spoon in one hand and a jar of peanut butter in the other.

Could this be her dinner, I wondered? No sooner had the thought popped into my head than I heard her mother's boyfriend snap, "Don't eat it all, Tiffany—you think you're the only one who's hungry?" He walked into view with two pieces of bread in hand, saw me, and slammed the door.

Peanut butter for dinner.

We started having Tiffany and her siblings over for dinner after that. They'd sit, wide-eyed, and watch while I lit candles and passed the basket of cloth napkins, and gape at Dave when he prayed over the meal. The first time Tiffany sat at our table, she grinned when Dave thanked the Lord for bringing her to our home.

All these new friends thrilled Zac, but he quickly learned these kids had been raised a bit differently than the Sunday school crowd back home.

"Tiffany said (*bleep*), Mom. What's that mean?"

Oh, boy, I'd think. I spent seven years trying to keep him from hearing that word, and now here it is.

Bedtime became de-programming time. I'd take a deep breath and plunge in. "Okay, Zac. What did you hear today?

A pattern emerged. The worst ideas came from Tiffany. The worst vocabulary came from Tiffany. The worst insults came from Tiffany.

I couldn't be sure if it was jealousy or just plain meanness, but for some reason Zac became her favorite target. She'd smile sweetly if he came to her door with Popsicles or gum, but if he showed up empty-handed he was likely to have the door slammed in his face.

"Who asked you to come over here?" she'd sneer.

I grew tired of seeing my son walk dejectedly back up the stairs. More and more frequently, I said no when he asked if Tiffany could come over. More and more often, I drove him across town to play with a new friend's children.

The final straw came one afternoon when Tiffany appeared at my door.

"My mom needs milk for the baby." She thrust a bottle toward me.

I rinsed the bottle and filled it with milk. Glancing at

41

Tiffany's dirty face, I thought for the hundredth time what a shame it was that no one ever thought to give her a bath. She had beautiful blue eyes and a broad, toothy grin that absolutely lit up her face. And that blonde hair. If they ever ran a brush through that hair...

"Oh, my word! Tiffany...you've got bugs in your hair!"

"No, I don't." She brushed a matted strand from her face.

"Oh, yes you do." Panic rose in me.

"Nope. My mom used that lice stuff on me and they're gone."

"Tiffany—I'm telling you, I can see them."

I handed her the bottle and escorted her to the door. "Tell your mother you need another treatment."

"I'm not tellin' her nothing." She stomped down the stairs.

I leaned over the railing. "Did she treat all you kids?"

"Nope. Just me. 'Cause I'm the only one who had 'em. And NOW...THEY'RE...GONE!" And so was she, slamming her front door behind her.

I didn't know her mother at all. Although I saw her nearly every day, it was always with a cigarette in one hand and the phone in the other. She'd stand just outside their front door for hours, smoking and talking on the phone. Occasionally she'd stop long enough to return my greeting, but we'd never had a real conversation. She wouldn't allow it. She felt free enough to send her kids up for borrowed milk, and had no problem letting them come for dinner or even to church with us, but there was a reserve about her that kept a distance between us.

I could only hope Tiffany passed on the message.

The following day, I discovered she had. "Hey—Zac's mom!" I heard floating up to the window. I leaned out and looked down.

Tiffany stood below our window with her hands on her hips. "My mom says it just takes a while. So there!" She

42

scampered back inside her apartment.

I sat for a minute before calling Zac to the kitchen.

"I don't want you playing with Tiffany for a while," I announced.

Take Tiffany with you.

The voice broke into my thoughts.

Take her with us? For the whole day? What madness had possessed me to have such a thought?

But then it occurred to me that I might not be arguing with myself. Maybe I was arguing with the Lord.

A minute of stewing convinced me. That whisper had to be heavenly, because there was no way on earth I'd ever make such a frightening suggestion to myself.

But Lord, I argued feebly, I don't see how one little car trip is going to have any impact on that child's life.

Take Tiffany with you.

It took a minute to explain the situation to Dave. He agreed I'd probably better stop arguing with the Lord and get myself downstairs to Tiffany's apartment. I swallowed hard on the walk down and prayed that God would send me two or three lice-deflecting angels.

I knocked as quietly as I could. Maybe they wouldn't hear. Or maybe they weren't home. Maybe she wouldn't...

"Yeah?" Tiffany's mom stood in the open door, holding a baby boy.

"Oh—hi. I don't know your name. I'm Shannon, Zac's mom."

She nodded. "Yeah, I know."

"I don't know your name," I repeated.

"Lori."

"Hi, Lori. Nice to finally meet you."

I shifted to my other foot. "I was wondering if Tiffany...if you...uh...We're going to Mt. St. Helens and thought maybe Tiffany would like to come."

Lori shrugged. "Fine by me."

She leaned back and hollered. When Tiffany appeared from down the hall, Lori said, "You want to go to Mt. St. Helens with them?"

Tiffany shrugged. "Guess so."

"Go find some shoes."

Lori nodded toward the living room and said, "You can wait in here if you want."

I followed her past the kitchen and into the living room. It took all my self-control not to show the alarm I felt. I'd never seen such a mess.

Piles of clothing covered every surface of the room and filled the baby's playpen to overflowing. Papers, toys, and fast-food wrappers littered the floor. The bit of carpet I could see under the debris was stained and crusty. Dirty diapers teetered in a haphazard pile. Ashtrays occupied the coffee table, end table, entertainment center, and television.

Lori nodded toward the couch. "There's some room there on the end."

She set the baby down and started folding clothes. I wanted to help, but didn't know how to offer without embarrassing her.

"I've been meaning to talk with you," she said.

"Oh?"

"I just wanted to say thanks."

That surprised me. "What for?"

She glanced toward a closed door down the hall. Lowering her voice, she answered, "For taking my kids to church."

We talked for forty-five minutes. She told me, shyly, that she used to go to church herself a long time ago, but then she had "fallen in with the wrong crowd" and left her church life behind. She said it was important to her that her kids went, but she was "too far gone" to take them herself. She said she didn't fit into all that anymore.

It was with a special joy that I got to tell her how wrong

she was. I got to tell her that it wasn't about church, or running with the right crowd, or fitting in. I got to share the one and only thing it all came down to: the grace of a Savior who stood in her place.

"Is that true?" she asked.

"It's true." I answered.

We took Tiffany to Mt. St. Helens. As I could have predicted, she wasn't very nice to Zac. Her insults were peppered with objectionable language. She demanded that we buy ice cream, then neglected to say thank you when we did. She elbowed him in the ribs on the way home.

But it hadn't been about Tiffany after all.

4

The Banjo Lady

"O LORD, you have examined my heart
    and know everything about me.
You know when I sit down or stand up.
    You know my every thought when far away.
You chart the path ahead of me
    and tell me where to stop and rest.
    Every moment you know where I am.
You know what I am going to say
    even before I say it, LORD....
Such knowledge is too wonderful for me."

—Psalm 139:1–6 (NLT)

Zac spotted her first. Maybe it was the color of her hair, which matched the soft whiteness of his grandmother's hair. Maybe it was her determination to take part in the contest, despite the fact that she needed an escort to help her up the aisle. I'm not sure what first caught his eye, but while I was busy sniffing the aroma of fritters and coffee, listening to the twang of fiddles and banjos, and watching taffeta dresses and flashy cowboy shirts sashay past, Zac centered his full attention on the lady in black.

I noticed something had changed when his bouncing stopped. Until then, he'd been a wiggling, jiggling, knee-tapping little monkey. As contestants made their brief appearances onstage and regaled us with tunes, Zac—himself a year-long veteran of violin lessons—couldn't resist playing along on his own air fiddle. I'd grown accustomed to his whole-body appreciation. So when his fingers and toes stilled suddenly, I followed the line of his gaze to see what had him so riveted.

She was elderly, as were most of the participants in this statewide competition. The dress she wore was taffeta, but simple. It lacked the sequins, rhinestones, and color of those worn by the other women. It hung so gently on her small frame that I was certain she wasn't wearing one of those crisp petticoats the others wore. As she inched past us, clutching the arm of her escort with one hand and a banjo in the other, the skirt of her dress rustled quietly like a whisper. Zac watched every step she took.

She glanced up as she passed, and I caught a glimpse of kind, brown eyes wreathed in beautiful laugh lines.

The escort supported her up and onto the platform. He waited while she settled herself on a chair, then turned and left her there in the center of the stage. Zac stared as she lifted the banjo to her lap and set her music on the stand.

She flashed a quick, shy smile toward the hundred or so people in the room, and even from the fourth row I could tell she was blushing. She lowered her eyes again and focused them on her music.

She wasn't the only banjo player we'd heard that night, and I can't honestly say she was the best. Her rendition of "Turkey in the Straw" was adequate, but not perfect. It wasn't a performance you'd call inspired or even memorable. But that was only my opinion. Zac seemed to hear something else, something I missed. His fascination never wavered, from her first twangy strum to her last; and when her brief song ended, he applauded with gusto.

The gentleman who had escorted her up came and helped her back down the stairs, then led her slowly to a

47

seat along the wall just a few feet from Zac's chair. Hanging on the cedar-planked wall behind her was a large black, white, and gray quilt. As she sank down on the bench, I couldn't help but notice how well her white hair and black dress blended into the quilt. The wall enveloped her. If she realized her invisibility, she didn't seem to mind.

She wasn't invisible to Zac, though. He kept watching her as one contestant after another took the stage. He was completely mesmerized by the woman. After several minutes, he turned around to me.

"Mom, do you have a piece of paper and a pencil?"

I dug through my purse and found both. "What do you need them for?" I couldn't resist asking.

"Just…something."

He rose slowly and walked toward the lady in black. She glanced up as he neared, and smiled, but looked away again as though she thought he would just walk past. When he didn't—when he stopped right in front of her—she turned her eyes toward him again.

I couldn't see his face, but I knew he was speaking to her. She leaned nearer. "What, honey?" I heard her ask.

He moved closer and bent his head toward hers.

"What?" This time it wasn't a matter of hearing. This time, it was a question of whether or not to believe what she had heard.

Zac held out the pencil and paper. An incredulous look came over the woman, and she blushed.

"Oh. Oh." She touched her heart, briefly, with one hand before taking the pencil.

She smoothed the paper carefully on the small table beside her bench. She glanced up again, once, as if to ask, "Are you sure?" And then she signed her name. With faltering hands, the banjo lady gave Zac the autograph he'd asked for.

He looked at the paper in his hand, turned, and scampered back to his seat. I'm not even sure he thanked her.

"Look, Mom!" He held his prize out for my approval.

Betty Russell, it said. The handwriting was shaky, but the "B" and the "R" had been written with big, flourishy letters.

Over Zac's shoulder, I watched a silver-haired woman in a snappy red and purple dress walk up and take a seat next to Betty. While she smoothed the folds of her billowy skirt, Betty leaned toward her and whispered. The two women giggled together. Betty tried to gesture furtively, casually, but I saw her point toward Zac. Both women turned soft gazes in his direction.

"Well, Betty, I guess this means you're a star now," the woman teased.

Betty blushed again. "I guess I am."

Zac clutched Betty's autograph all the way home, and as soon as we opened the front door of the house, he shot down the hall to his bedroom. I assumed he was going to stash it in his pirate treasure chest, along with all his other important bounty—baseball cards, oddly-shaped rocks, old bottle caps, a screw-driver with a broken tip, candy wrappers. I figured Betty's autograph would just be added to the collection.

But that's not exactly what happened. What happened— exactly—is that he folded that paper into an airplane the next morning and threw it at our dog.

I was looking out our front window when he did it. He just sat down on the porch steps, folded the airplane—lickety-split, just like his dad had taught him—and called out to our dog.

"Hey, Bear! Watch out for planes!"

And away the thing went, soaring through the sky—and missing the dog by about six inches. Bear gave Zac a "Can't you do better than that?" look and waddled back around the side of the house.

I didn't know until I went outside and stooped to pick it

up that he'd used Betty's autograph to make the airplane. There, on the wing, was her name. "Betty Ru" was all I could make out.

I walked back to the porch and sat down on the third step. How sad, I thought, that one day you're riding at the top, soaking in applause and signing autographs, and the next day someone decides your autograph would make a great paper airplane.

I could still see the look of disbelief on Betty's face when Zac whispered his request. "Me?!" her expression asked. All it took was one small boy and one wrinkled piece of paper, and suddenly the modest wallflower was transformed into a star. His simple gesture made her feel significant, and noticed—maybe for the first time in a long time. She was clearly not a person used to that kind of attention. She was clearly not someone accustomed to being pulled out of the crowd.

I wasn't quite sure why this incident bothered me so, except that I kept seeing the astonishment in her eyes when Betty realized someone had taken the time to really see her. I didn't know how long it would be in her life before she felt that way again. It broke my heart.

But then, God whispered.

I *see her.*

I *never stop looking at her.*

I *watch over her when she's sleeping.*

She's *the apple of My eye.*

She *matters to Me, and she's not invisible…I see her.*

Then, as I stared down at the autograph in my hand, He brought His words to me from Isaiah: "See, I *have engraved you on the palm of My hands."*

The thought was too incredible. My name—and Betty's, too—was engraved in a place of permanence and prominence. It wasn't written on paper, which can be torn or crumpled. It was not carved in wood or chiseled on stone. Those

We hadn't gone far before Zac grew independent. Dropping my hand, he forged ahead, slowing down only long enough to grab a skinny stick he spied in the brush. He was the first explorer in a new land, whacking ferns and smacking nettles, poking in bushes and burrows, plowing a footpath.

I let him lead, but I watched him closely. And I reveled in the sight. Sun-speckles danced on his brown curls as he strutted along in front of me. His eyes drank the forest. Every bend in the path brought new delights, new exclamations. When he "oohed" over a discovered mushroom, I bent down with him and watched his little fingers squeeze the helpless fungus to pieces. When he "aahed" over a stinkweed, I bent down again and let him shove it behind my ear. The woods resounded with squeals and laughter.

While we walked, we talked about all the really important things in life. He explained to me why people who make brownies should never put nuts in them; I explained why it's not a good idea to put the cat's tail in your mouth. We swapped favorite colors. We marched like soldiers. He sang a song from *The Little Mermaid*. He told me the only joke he knew; I pretended not to have heard it from him before.

As we came around a giant oak tree, Zac stopped in his tracks and shuddered. He turned and looked up at me.

"You go first, Mama."

I looked over his head and saw an enormous spider web suspended across the path. While he waited from a safe distance, I found my own stick—a heftier, Mom-sized version of his skinny twig—and whacked the web apart.

He liked the new arrangement. I kept at my task as we continued our walk. Where spider webs crisscrossed between bushes and trees, I swung my mighty stick and made the woods safe for him. Where the brush was thick, I stepped and smooshed and cleared a path for us both.

He followed, carefree, like the little prince he is. When he

53

grew hungry, I pulled a granola bar from my pocket. I even took the wrapper off for him. When he complained of thirst, I gave him a swig from my sports bottle. He guzzled wildly, then handed the bottle back for me to carry. And when, inevitably, he yawned and slowed his pace, I picked him up and turned us both toward home—despite all his crabby protestations.

While we retraced our steps, I let my eyes take in the beauty all around us. Scattered throughout the forest, tall timbers rose like columns in an emerald cathedral. The incense in this temple was a mingling of moss and pine, dying leaves and moist earth. The choir consisted of trilling birds, chattering squirrels, and the snap and crumble of crisp leaves and twigs beneath my feet. Reverence hushed me.

We were about halfway home when Zac spotted a circle of small pinecones beneath a lofty hemlock. Momentarily revived, he wriggled out of my arms and ran to fill his pockets.

A sun shaft broke through the branches of an oak tree and blanketed a fallen log next to Zac's hemlock. I accepted the invitation and settled myself on the mossy seat. While he piled the pinecones in haphazard pyramids and practiced his counting, I rested.

Still far from the house, my troubles were dwarfed by the splendor of the forest. I could forgive my friend. No doubt she'd call back and tell me why she had been so snippy. The money would eventually be found for the bill we owed. Dave would figure out what was making the noise in the car and fix it. He always did. The chocolate chips…well, those weren't even worth worrying about.

It all seemed so insignificant from where I sat, under those towering trees, staring up at the shards of blue sky breaking through the green ceiling above. I sat and wished I could always have this perspective.

I looked at Zac, squatted down next to his treasures. He had no worries, other than how best to carry home a pound of pinecones. He'd had no worries all day. All his needs, on this little jaunt, had been met by me. I fed him, carried him, and watched over him. He didn't bother wondering whether or not we were heading in the right direction. He just enjoyed my company and trusted I'd work out all the details.

He was wise, that boy. The minute something scary or overwhelming popped up, he knew just where to turn, and just what to say. "You go first, Mama."

On a breeze that rippled the barely-clinging leaves overhead, I heard the Lord whisper.

Wouldn't you like to let Me go first?

The question startled me. Had I been running ahead?

He showed me a glimpse of His daughter: little, independent me—confident of my direction and sure of my strength. He let me see myself trying to beat a path through the woods without Him, unaware of how closely He hovered.

And He let me see His heart, which longed to make the path for me. Longed to provide the food I craved and the water I thirsted for. Longed to heal my hurts.

I understood the lesson. He wanted what I wanted—to meet all the needs of my child and keep all the scary things away.

"I'll try, Father," I whispered back.

Zac's eyes were closed when we emerged from the forest. His breath felt warm on my neck. The pinecones bulging from his pockets scratched against my arm, but I didn't mind. I loved the weight and substance of my child, sleeping in my arms.

Remembering my promise, I stopped on the porch steps before walking through the doorway, and took a moment to make a suggestion.

"You go first, Father."

Autumn

"A time to mend…a time to gather"

Three years running, Tera pestered us to let her get baptized. Every time our church gathered on the shores of Lake Stevens with our towels and guitars—regardless of whether it was in the heat of July or the chill of February—Tera made her case anew. "I'm ready now. Let me get in there with everybody else!" The problem was, she never could quite convince us she understood what all the fuss was about. She just wanted some of that fuss for herself.

But this summer—her eighth—things finally came together. When Tera approached us this time, she spoke matter-of-factly. "I've been reading my Bible. It says that when you believe that Jesus is your Savior, you're supposed to get baptized. So how 'bout it?"

It just isn't possible to argue with that kind of logic. We didn't even try.

The night before the big event, however, Tera started worrying. She'd had time to reflect on all the baptisms she'd witnessed over the years, and it brought up a few questions. She decided it might be wise to have a little pre-baptism consultation with the pastor. So she went to his office.

"Dad?"

He looked up from his books.

"I was wondering something."

He cleared off a spot for her on the chair next to his desk. "What are you wondering?"

She settled herself on the chair. "Well, it's this: when you dunk me tomorrow, how long are you going to hold me under?"

"Not long at all. Just a second or two."

She exhaled in relief. "Oh, boy. That's good to hear. 'Cause you know, I can't hold my breath for very long."

He tried not to laugh. This was a serious consultation, after all.

"Is that it?"

She shook her head. "There's one other thing," she said.

"What's that?"

"Well, I was wondering…how far out are you going to take me? I mean, are we going out past the docks?"

"Oh, no," Dave said. "We won't go out that far. We'll only go about halfway out."

Tera nodded. "Good. 'Cause you know, Dad, I'm pretty short."

"I've noticed," he said, grinning.

She stood up to leave. "Tera?" Dave stopped her.

She turned to look at him.

"You don't have to worry. I've got the whole thing planned out for you. All you have to do is show up, okay?"

She took his words to heart. In fact, Tera was so carefree and unconcerned the next morning that she didn't bother bringing a change of clothes or a towel. But that was okay. We had it covered—it's our job.

God has a job, too. It's to protect you, to provide for all your needs, to make sure that one day runs into another and your heart keeps a steady rhythm and you have all the air you need to breathe. His shoulders are big and His arms are long. There's nothing you need that He can't provide, whether it's finances, health, a comforting word, or even a bottle of corn syrup (chapter seven will clear that one up).

We have only one job, and that's to hold His hand. That's it. Under "Duties and responsibilities of the child of God," there's just a single line written: "Hold tight." The minute we let go is the minute all the stewing and fretting begins. We start panicking, and the next thing you know, we're off trying to run our lives again. His hand is still there—open, waiting—but we don't notice because we're too busy trying to keep all the bad things at bay. We're swatting at foes, both real and imagined, and scanning the skies for approaching storms.

It's all so unnecessary. The fix is simple: walk back to Jesus and put your hand in His. Start trusting again. Rest.

Two of the most important people in my life were my maternal grandparents, Clifford and Mickey. Watching their lives, I learned everything I needed to know about affection and commitment, patience, honor, humor, and the importance of a good work ethic. But I have one memory of my grandparents that surpasses all others and sums up the beauty of their love for one another.

I walked into the house early one evening to find the heavy, wonderful scent of bacon hanging in the air and Grandpa cooking eggs at the stove. "Grandma had a hankering for breakfast, so that's what we're having for dinner," he explained.

Though only sixty, Grandma was confined to a wheelchair. "Old Arthur," as she called her rheumatoid arthritis, had nearly crippled her. On good days, she could get around the house a bit, but during especially bad spells, she was completely dependent on the rest of us.

Grandpa was a big, burly John Wayne-of-a-man who owned a dump truck and spent long hours hauling gravel for his customers. He was a hard worker—the hardest I've ever known—and the man I most admired in the world. I could tell he'd just gotten home from work, because he hadn't yet taken off his boots, but he knew Grandma was hungry and he saw to her needs first.

"I'll pour a cup of coffee for her," I offered.

"Not yet, darlin'," he said. "You know Grandma only likes it piping hot. Wait until her food is ready."

I waited. When he dished up her bacon, eggs, and toast and set her plate and a folded napkin on a tray, I poured a cup and followed him into their bedroom.

I'm pretty sure she saw me right off, but she only had eyes for Grandpa in that first second. She looked at the tray in his big truck-driver hands and then settled her pretty eyes on his face.

"Oh, Clifford," she said, with a tender smile, "you're my protector and my provider."

There never was a love story quite like theirs. Unless, of course, you count the love story between you and your Savior. It's a similar tale: helpless woman completely dependent, for all her needs and wants, on the One who adores her. Safe in His arms. Assured of His protection. And oh, so loved.

In the autumns of our lives, we've somehow forgotten how big the hands of God really are. We think and fret and scheme until we've worn ourselves out with worry. And all the time, God is there, whispering, "Let Me take care of you."

These autumn stories describe moments of revelation, encouragement, provision, and protection. As you read through these chapters, ask your Father to show you yourself in these stories. Are you busying yourself with unimportant things, forgetting the one needful thing? Are you exhausted from trying to hold onto the past, blind to what you're missing today? Are you in need of sheltering arms in the midst of a storm?

God is waiting to be your Protector and Provider. Let Him.

6

Jellybeans and Marshmallows

"Learn as you go along what pleases the Lord."
—Ephesians 5:10 (TLB)

Warm, moist breath floated across my cheek, and with it, a strong sugary smell. Reluctantly, I lifted my weary eyelids to find two wide, mischievous green eyes staring down at me from a height of about four inches.

"Good. You're awake," Zac pronounced, in a voice at least ten decibels louder than I would ever care to hear that early in the morning. It didn't help that his mouth was mere inches from my ear.

"Zac," I muttered thickly, "I smell sugar. Have you been in the sugar?"

"Nope. I made you a surprise."

He was only five, so the words "I made" caused my heart to beat a bit faster. If I was just waking up and Dave had already left for work, then that meant Mr. Crafty had no supervision at all while he "made" whatever it was he made. I assessed the possibilities: had it involved a glue gun? Paint? A chainsaw?

"Oops!" he said. Two soft, round orbs bounced off my head and onto the pillow. "I'm spilling your surprise."

I turned my head and stared at the two marshmallows on my bed. "You made me something with marshmallows?"

61

"Aren't you excited?" He lowered the plate I hadn't noticed him holding high above my head. It was big, heavy, and stoneware—and I felt suddenly thankful to be hit by marshmallows and not the plate itself.

"It's breakfast in bed!" He plopped the plate onto my unprepared stomach, spilling yet another marshmallow.

I sat up slowly and surveyed the feast. "Oh, Zac, you shouldn't have!" I meant it more than he could know. There they were—all his favorites, sitting right on my plate. A handful of chocolate chips next to a handful of jellybeans. Two tootsie rolls. A graham cracker with a dollop of whipped cream (artfully done, I must add). Six sugar cubes. And, of course, the marshmallows.

"Oops! I forgot your coffee! I'll be right back." He scurried out of the room, leaving me to ponder his gift.

My first realization was that we needed to install a lock for the pantry. The second—and more sobering—thought was that I was going to have to eat some of that stuff or Zac would be disappointed. I weighed my options as I heard his footsteps returning, then quickly scooped up the jellybeans and deposited them in my pillowcase.

"Here you go!" He set a mug on my nightstand and watched proudly as I picked it up.

Ahh, morning coffee, I thought naively. Maybe I'd be able to get through this. Then I took the first sip. Ahh, yesterday's coffee, I corrected, shuddering from the impact of ice cold liquid slithering down my throat. Of course it's from yester-day, I realized. What had I been thinking? Zac didn't know how to make coffee yet. I made a mental note to teach him how, right after…breakfast.

He rounded the bed and hopped onto the other side. It was clear he was going to watch me take every last sip and nibble. I had to find a way to get him out of the room. "Aren't you going to have some?" I asked hopefully.

"Already ate. It's good, isn't it?"

"Oh…yes, honey. But you know, it's really the thought that counts, don't you think?"

"What's that mean?"

"It means that…well, the best part of this breakfast is the fact that you took the time to make it, and…it's not the eating part that's so special, it's the…uh…the…"

"Hey, what's this?" Four or five renegade jellybeans escaped and rolled out of the pillowcase.

"Well, now. That's funny," I said with an uncomfortable laugh. "I guess they slipped off my plate."

"I'll get 'em for you, Mom."

And he did. Every last one. As he settled in to enjoy my predicament, I began the task. I took a bite. I made appropriately appreciative noises. I fought the revulsion.

I was touched at Zac's thoughtfulness, but I was also surprised. Hadn't my darling son been watching me every morning of his five years? Didn't he know me better than this? Mornings for me consist of coffee, and maybe more coffee, but almost never food, and certainly never sugar.

Out of nowhere, sitting there on the bed trying to choke down my son's offering, a thought struck me. Did I ever give God breakfast in bed—figuratively speaking? Did I ever load His plate with all my favorites, and beam with pride as I presented it to Him? Did I know Him well enough that I offered things pleasing to Him, or did I only offer gifts that pleased and delighted me?

The question made me squirm just a tad, and I couldn't help but wonder—what was I about to load on His plate this morning? I knew I had a full schedule. First off, I had to teach Zac how to make coffee. Then I had a writer's group meeting at ten. I needed to go to the post office. I had two big crates of recycling to drop off. Several women were coming that afternoon to work on crafts. I wanted to get at least a bit of exercise in there somewhere. Oh, and a quiet time.

Hmmm. I reviewed my list, and all the "I needs" and "I

wants" popped right out at me. My quiet time nearly suffocated there at the bottom, under all the other "have to's."

I could sense the Lord waiting for me to explain.

"But, Lord," I began to argue, "You know these aren't frivolous things. It's good that Zac learns new skills, right? And...our craft time has become a ministry, almost an outreach to the neighbor ladies, and...and...You want me to recycle, don't You, Lord?

Heaven was silent. I had a sudden picture of God choking on one of the marshmallows I just offered Him. "Please hurry and swallow, Lord—I need to hear what You'd rather have this morning."

He whispered through familiar words from the Book of Luke: *Martha, Martha, you are worried and bothered about so many things; but only a few things are necessary, really only one...*

"Hey, Mom—how come you're not eating?"

I had nearly forgotten my little breakfast warden. "Oh, you know, sweetie, I'm getting so full. How 'bout if we save the rest of this to give to Daddy when he gets home?" Heh, heh.

"Yeah! He'll love it!" Zac scooped up my plate. "Want to finish your coffee?"

"No, no!" I responded a bit too forcefully. "You can take that, too."

He started toward the door. "Are you glad I made you breakfast in bed, Mom?"

"Oh, honey, I'm gladder than you could know."

He grinned. "Well, I was going to make you new coffee, but I didn't know how."

"That's okay, Zac, 'cause I meant what I said earlier. It really is the thought that counts. But I was thinking, maybe we can do something about that. How about if later today I teach you how to use the coffeemaker?"

"Yeah!" He was clearly up for that challenge. "But let's do it right now!"

I considered for one second explaining to my son that God was waiting for His breakfast in bed, but I thought better of it. "Later, honey. I promise."

The door closed. I slipped out of bed and dropped to my knees.

Yes, I mused, the thought counts—but the gift matters, too.

7

Little Things

"*Delight yourself in the* LORD
and he will give you the desires of your heart."

—Psalm 37:4

At first, it all just seemed like a big adventure. In the middle of his ninth year of employment at the local paper mill, Dave came home one day and announced that God had been speaking to him about going into the ministry. He said, in fact, that he'd been having an ongoing conversation with the Lord over the course of two years—and it was time to answer the call. I gave his bombshell pronouncement a split second's worth of consideration, nodded my agreement, and waited for further instructions. He pointed out that he'd have to quit his job. I was okay with that. He reminded me that we'd be living on practically nothing while he attended seminary. I was okay with that too. I decided to let the whole thing roll off me. I made up my mind not to worry about the unknowns ahead of us. After all, if God was in this thing, He'd take care of the details. I figured all the truly hard work belonged to Him—we simply had to follow.

As far as I could tell, the role being offered me was that of "cheerful partner-slash-cheerleader." So I set myself to the task. I assessed our situation and brought my findings to Dave for consideration. Living in Latte Land the way we do (the greater Seattle area), we had developed a pretty decent Starbucks addiction. So right off the bat, we cut our frequent latte stops down to one a week. When our finances tightened up further, we apologized to our favorite barista and stopped going altogether. I learned to make semi-passable lattes at home instead.

We adopted other frugal living habits. I began making bread from scratch. That first summer, I planted a big vegetable garden and canned dozens of jars of jam from the wild blackberries growing all around our farm. We stopped going out to eat. I started sewing again. Instead of renting movies at the video store, we hunted for good children's movies at the library. When we grew bored with their selection, we began listening to classic books on tape. And through all that, it was still fun.

When Dave's train commute to his classes in Portland grew tedious, we made the decision to leave our farm and move to an apartment closer to campus. My one worry was leaving my garden, which I saw as a source of nearly free food, but God had that covered. A committee of professors' wives—taking pity on the struggling seminary students— stocked a basement room with used clothing, canned goods, dry beans, and an assortment of macramé potholders, chipped cups, fondue pots, and other mismatched houseware items. The inventory, I learned, remained pretty constant. The same orange and green crocheted doily I saw on my first visit was still there on my last, more than a year later. Unless someone thought to leave a bag of split peas instead of the usual brown or white beans, nothing much changed. But "The Wear-House," as it was called, was our own private thrift store—and it was all free. We were encouraged to take as much as we needed. I became a regular down in the basement, and though I had pretty much memorized the goods by the first week, it still gave me a thrill to walk downstairs and peek inside.

Things went along just fine there in our little apartment for a good seven months, right up until the end of November. Early in the week of Thanksgiving, a thoughtful Portland butcher donated twenty-five care boxes to the seminary and asked that the food be distributed according to need. Part of the bounty came our way. My heart was full as I surveyed our box. We'd been blessed with a turkey, an assortment of sausages, a ham for Christmas dinner, some pork chops, and even a few small steaks. There was meat enough to stretch over several weeks.

Our food budget was so limited that I hadn't been buying much meat at all. We ate a lot of beans and rice, potatoes and eggs, and on occasion, casseroles made with the cheapest turkey legs I could find. But here was a big box of meat. Steak, even! I felt a rush of gratitude.

"Thank You, Lord," I said out loud.

I hadn't noticed Zac standing behind me. "Why are you saying 'Thank You, Lord'?" he asked.

I grinned. "Because He always provides just what we need."

Thursday afternoon, after filling ourselves with turkey, the three of us went our separate ways. Dave headed to the couch for a nap. Zac went next door to play with his friend. I walked down to our storage unit to find our Christmas boxes. It was a tradition. In my mind, the very second Thanksgiving dinner was over, we moved officially into Christmas.

I lugged the first box up to the apartment and emptied it. The crèche went on the mantle, along with Mary, Joseph, and the animals. The manger and baby Jesus went in our bedroom; they wouldn't go into the crèche until Christmas morning. I set the Wise Men near the front door. They'd move slowly toward the mantel as the weeks went by.

The wooden holly sprig went on the wall near the kitchen. The "Let It Snow" plaque went on the front door. Baskets found their way on top of shelves and desks and end tables.

By the time Dave woke from his nap and Zac returned home, the apartment was transformed. But I had made a mistake, and I realized it immediately.

"Dave, I wasn't thinking when I packed our stuff. I left all our Christmas music at home—and all the puzzles."

"Hmm." He liked the music as much as I did. We had a big box of CDs we'd collected over the years. My tradition was to buy one new CD of instrumental Christmas music every year. We played our favorites all through the season, but we looked forward to finding new favorites, too. When I'd packed a few boxes to bring with us to seminary, I packed carefully. Not realizing how tight our finances would actually be, I had simply counted on buying a new CD when Christmas rolled around, so I'd left all the rest in storage.

We also bought one new puzzle each Christmas. Zac was old enough now to help put it together, and visitors always liked placing a piece or two when they dropped by. I left all those puzzles back home as well—figuring I'd follow my tradition and buy a new one.

"I just didn't think about how tight things would be," I explained. I waited only a split second before asking, "Do you think we can get a new puzzle and a CD this year?"

He thought for a long minute. I could see he didn't want to disappoint me. But finally he shook his head. "Sorry, Shanny. I don't see how we can this year."

A lump appeared in my throat. I didn't want to argue. I knew it wasn't his fault we were so strapped. I also knew the CD and the puzzle didn't matter to anyone else nearly as much as it mattered to me. Friends often teased me about attaching too much importance to traditions. But I believed it was my job to anchor memories for my family. Traditions did that. I knew when Zac was a dad himself, he'd tell his children about how we always had homemade cinnamon rolls on the day of the first snowfall every winter. He'd tell them about "Nick and Nancy," the twins none of us had ever seen, but who came and went secretly, leaving goody baskets and notes on our doorstep before knocking and disappearing into the night. He'd make sure Nick and Nancy left goodies for his own children.

And at Christmas, I wanted him to describe the scene we enjoyed every year: lots of homemade yummies. Candles and wreaths. A puzzle on the table for visitors to help put together. And always—in the background—beautiful music.

I went into the kitchen to start a pot of turkey soup. As I chopped the tiny bit of onion I'd managed to save, and cut my one carrot into little pieces and threw them into the pot, I decided—for the first time—that it really wasn't very much fun being a trooper.

I moped around all the next day. Dave could tell I was upset; he apologized another time or two. I told him I understood. I told him I wasn't mad. And I really wasn't mad—at him. I was simply mad that I'd hit a wall. Frustrated that I'd come across the one thing I couldn't smile away. I grieved over that lost music, that missing puzzle. Even as I told myself it was silly and reminded myself of all the blessings we'd been given, all the important needs God had filled, I still found myself mourning my traditions.

Late that afternoon, I reached into the cupboard to get the garlic salt. Someone—Dave, no doubt—had put it up on the top shelf. I got a chair and stood on it to reach the jar. As I pulled it off the shelf, I noticed a bag of Spanish peanuts hiding behind the toothpicks.

"Where'd those come from?" I asked out loud. I hadn't bought any peanuts. I hadn't brought them with me from home, either. And Dave never set foot in the grocery store.

I didn't really care where they came from, because suddenly, I felt better. Dave loved peanut brittle. I didn't have much in the way of baking supplies this year, but I could surprise him and make peanut brittle. I looked through the cupboard again. I had just enough sugar, but I'd need to get corn syrup.

I hopped down off the chair and ran to check my purse. I only had a few dollars left of grocery money, but I couldn't imagine corn syrup being very expensive. I'd just get a small bottle.

"Dave, I need to run to the store. Do you mind?"

He came out of the bedroom. "Nope. Can you pick something up for me while you're out?" he asked.

I nodded.

He handed me four dollars. "I have to turn in a report tomorrow, but the printer is out of paper. Just pick up the cheapest package of copy paper you can find."

"No problem."

"Oh," he added, walking behind me toward the door, "and we're out of milk. I just finished the last of it."

I stopped at that. Paper *and* milk? What about the corn syrup?

He dug through his pocket and pulled out two quarters, which he handed to me. "Just do your best. Maybe the paper won't be that expensive."

I worried all the way to the office supply store. Once there, I read the price of every last package of paper before settling on the cheapest. I had just a little over four dollars with me when I left.

The office supply store was across the parking lot from a grocery store and toy store. I left my car and walked across the parking lot. Though I intended to go right to the grocery store, I couldn't help but veer off to the toy store. I knew I didn't have enough money for a puzzle, but I just had to look. Maybe they had a very cheap puzzle in a bargain bin.

They didn't. Even the least expensive of their puzzles cost more than what I had in my purse.

When I pushed the door to the grocery store open, the first thing I saw was a huge display of CDs, right in the front of the store. I rushed to look. The majority of the CDs were Christmas music, and several were instrumental, but there wasn't a single CD priced below seven dollars.

I swallowed my disappointment and headed to the back of the store. At least there'd be peanut brittle. Dave would be surprised and it would still seem somewhat like our usual Christmas.

I went to get the milk first. They were having a sale—I got a gallon for two dollars. That left two dollars for corn syrup. Surely they'd have a small size in that price range.

But when I stood in the baking aisle and looked at my choices, my heart sunk. I had two sizes of corn syrup to choose from, and the smallest cost $2.99.

I stared at those bottles, willing them to become cheaper. I must have stood there five minutes, just looking at the row of bottles I couldn't afford to buy.

It was going to have to be one or the other. Either I came home with corn syrup, or I came home with milk.

I didn't start crying until I'd set the gallon of milk in the car beside me and shut my door. But I cried all the way back to the apartment, as rain pelted my windshield and all my Christmas joy washed away.

I was quiet the rest of that week. Dave noticed. "I'm driving over to the campus to turn in a paper. Why don't you and Zac come with me?"

I didn't want to go. He could tell, but he insisted—which wasn't like him at all. "You need to get out of the apartment. C'mon. Zac, go get your coat."

When we reached the seminary parking lot, he said, "Zac, you come with me to see my professor. We'll let Mom have some time to herself."

"I don't mind going with you two," I said.

"No, I think you need to take a walk. Why don't you go over to The Wear-House and see what's new?"

"There's never anything new," I said. But I hadn't been

there in several weeks, so I took his suggestion. I turned and sauntered across the grass, kicking wet leaves and feeling sorry for myself.

The building seemed completely empty. My steps echoed against the walls as I made my way downstairs. When I pushed open the door to The Wear-House, the room was pitch black. I groped for the switch just inside the doorway and flipped it on. The second the light illuminated the darkness, I was reminded of how much God loves me.

My eyes were drawn instantly to the cupboard directly in front of where I stood. The same bags of beans sat on the bottom shelf. The same cans of corn sat on the middle shelf. But on the top shelf, sitting there all by its lonesome, God had left a gift for me: a single bottle of corn syrup.

I flew across the room and reached up on tiptoes to grab the bottle. It was real. The syrup inside slogged slowly against the glass when I tipped it to one side. I held it to my chest and hugged it.

I hadn't asked. Not once during the week had I bothered to ask God for that corn syrup. But He gave it to me anyway.

"Oh, Father...thank You. Thank You for seeing that I wanted this little thing and for making a way for me to have it."

I turned to go. I couldn't wait to tell Dave. I couldn't wait to explain the reason for my mopeyness, to tell him how God saw it all and knew how much those small things meant to me.

But I didn't quite make it out of the room. Halfway to the door, my glance fell on a box I'd never seen there before. It still had a price tag on it, it was still shrink-wrapped, and it was one of the most beautiful puzzles I'd ever laid eyes on.

"Oh, Lord," I whispered.

I picked it up and shook my head in amazement. He loved me so much.

And then I walked to the door and lifted my hand to turn

off the light switch. For some reason, I glanced down at the last second. There, on the table next to the door, I saw a single CD. A CD of Christmas music—*instrumental* Christmas music.

I just leaned against the door and cried.

In the stillness of that room, I heard my Father's voice.

Daughter, it is My joy to surprise you—and My delight to delight you.

We ate the peanut brittle. Dave loved it. When the corn syrup bottle was empty, I washed it out and dried it. I wrote down this story and rolled it in a scroll, tied a ribbon around the middle, and dropped it in the bottle. Many similar stories have been added to that bottle over the years, each one a reminder of the whisper I heard in the darkness.

I had been wrong in the kitchen that day with Zac, when I'd told him, "God always provides just what we need." The truth is, He provides abundantly more than "just what we need." In His quest to show us how much He loves us, our Father brings us daily surprises and unexpected pleasures.

I've learned to watch for those little things.

8

No Fair

"When we were utterly helpless with no way of escape, Christ came at just the right time and died for us sinners who had no use for him. Even if we were good, we really wouldn't expect anyone to die for us....But God showed his great love for us by sending Christ to die for us while we were still sinners."

—Romans 5:6–8 (TLB)

When Zac was four, a couple we barely knew asked if their ten-year-old daughter could live with us for an indefinite time. We'd never considered fostering before, but we knew this couple was in the midst of some serious family problems, so we prayed. The answer God gave us was "yes." I looked forward to having a girl in the house. I tried to anticipate the changes her presence might bring, and I thought I was prepared for the adventure, at least mentally. But one change caught me completely by surprise.

About a week after Ashley joined our family—making me no longer the mother of an only child but suddenly the mother of siblings—a friend asked if we needed anything. I'm sure she meant clothing, or furniture for Ashley's bedroom. But I had a different suggestion.

"If you really want to help, could you get me some accurate measuring devices? One of those science beaker thingies with milliliter marks along the side, or maybe a balancing scale?"

She paused a long moment before asking, "And you need those things for…?"

"For measuring out the kids' snacks and juice. You know. To make sure I'm being fair."

She thought that was funny. In fact, she apparently thought I was joking, because she didn't get me the beaker *or* the scale. I had to just continue eyeballing the weights and measurements of all the kids' snacks. And according to the two of them, I was a terrible estimator.

"Hey—no fair! She's got more applesauce than me!"

"Oh yeah? Well, the frosting on your cake is thicker than mine. That's even more not fair."

I'd run back to the kitchen and grab more of this or that, hoping to appease the little fairness judges.

I began pouring juice near the window where the light was best. I'd pour carefully, then squat down and scrutinize the levels. Three more drops in the left glass; one more in the right. When all looked perfect, I'd cross my fingers and try to control my trembling as I carried the offering to the prince and princess. Then, like a good serf, I'd wait for their pronouncement.

I nearly always failed. If it wasn't a matter of measurement, it was a matter of who got the better glass, the cleanest fork, or the more perfectly-shaped ice cubes. I simply couldn't win.

M&Ms were a nightmare. That first time, I wasn't thinking at all. I just reached in the bag and pulled out a handful for each child. They went to work, analyzing and comparing their respective piles with near-computer swiftness.

Zac fell silent, a mischievous grin spreading across his otherwise cherubic face. Ashley whimpered as if she'd been kicked.

"No fair. He has six more than me."

So I learned. The next time, I counted their candy, much the way a pharmacist counts pills.

76

Five, ten, fifteen for Zac. Five, ten, fifteen for Ashley.

That satisfied them both. For about three seconds.

"No fair!" they cried in unison.

"Wrong!" I protested. "Wrong! I counted this time—*carefully*!"

"But he has more green."

"Well, she has more red."

Defeated, I crawled to the phone and called a friend.

"Carol, help. Help me," I gasped.

"Shannon? What's wrong?"

I pulled myself up to a chair. "They're driving me crazy. Everything...and I mean *everything*...has to be fair."

Carol laughed. "Oh, that. All siblings do that. You just never dealt with it before, because Zac was an only child." Mike and Carol had already raised four children, so I figured she knew what she was talking about.

"You're my lifeline. Tell me your secret. What did you do? How did you cope? How did you survive?"

"I had a comeback. Whenever one of my children said 'No fair' to something, I'd just answer 'The Fair is in September.'"

I liked that idea. I tried it, first chance I got.

Not twenty minutes after my conversation with Carol, Ashley discovered Zac had been given one and a half milliliters more grape juice than she had.

"No fair!" she argued.

I drew a deep breath for courage. "Um...the uh...the Fair is in September."

"What?"

I tried again more boldly. "I said...I said that the Fair is in September."

Ashley turned to Zac. "Do you know what she's talking about?"

"I think she means the Fair with all the cows and corn dogs and rides."

"Oh, I love the Fair! Are we going?"

Zac nodded. "We always go. I always get a corn dog and two scones and a big bag of cotton candy."

Ashley clapped her hands. "I'm going to have three scones. I love scones."

"No fair! Then I want three scones, too."

I ran to my bedroom and hit the speed dial.

"Carol—it didn't work! They still think everything's unfair!"

"Oh, it's only temporary," she clarified. "It's kind of like sticking a teeny little wrench in a giant cog. It only stops the machine long enough for you to make a quick exit. Hey! You got to your bedroom, right? Be thankful."

There was no winning the battle. So I began to retreat. Dave called from work one afternoon and asked what we were all doing.

"Oh, you know. This and that," I whispered.

"Why are you whispering?"

"I'm…I'm in the bedroom closet. I don't want them to hear me."

"Why are you in the closet?"

A whimper escaped. "Because they're out there…and they want a snack."

Silence.

"Did you hear? They want a snack. Worse than that, they want M&Ms!"

More silence.

"I can't take it anymore, I tell you! I can't take it! I'm sick of the endless counting. Four red for her, four red for him…it never stops!"

"So don't count."

"What?!" Had he gone mad?

"Just stick your hand in the bag and pull out a fistful for each of them."

I gasped. "It doesn't work like that…they'd never agree!"

Dave laughed. "You're the mom. Enjoy your power. Just

78

tell them: 'You get what you're given.'"

I could barely speak the words at first, for fear that they'd be heard from the other side of the door. But I kept practicing. Dave worked with me. After several minutes, I felt the first small blush of confidence.

"I'm ready."

"I'll be praying for you."

I opened the closet door, opened the bedroom door, and ran straight to the bag of M&Ms. Thrusting my hand inside, I turned to Zac and Ashley, waiting at the kitchen table.

"You get what you're given! You get what you're given!"

I tossed them each a handful of candy and ran straight back to my bedroom.

Of course, I couldn't stay there forever. Eventually, I left my haven and returned to the battle. I held my ground, small though it was, and made steady advances. The kids got so tired of my hysterical cries of "The Fair's in September!" and "You get what you're given!" that they eventually decided, in the name of peace and tranquility, to just gracefully accept whatever they were tossed.

And then one night, right in the middle of our bedtime tucking-in routine, Zac shook his head. "It's not fair at all, Mom."

Oh, here we go again. What now? I wondered. Had Ashley breathed more than her share of air today? Received one more hug than he?

"What?" I asked, not really wanting to know the answer.

"Jesus."

Now he had my attention.

"What's not fair about Jesus?"

Zac glanced down at his Bible, which we had just been reading together.

"He shouldn't have been up on that cross. He didn't do anything wrong. Not anything."

Zac's eyes watered. Mine did, too.

"It's not fair, Mom. That should have been me on the cross."

I kissed him and we said our prayers together. I was still praying when I closed his door and stepped out on our back porch.

I looked up at the black velvet sky and replayed Zac's words. "He didn't do anything...that should have been me."

And I thought about the ultimate unfairness: God on a cross. Perfect, sinless God—in my place.

If everything were fair, all my iniquities past, present, and future would be stored in some giant celestial vat, waiting to drown me when I reached the end of my sin-filled life. Instead, the vat was emptied by my Savior. Instead, I've been given the right to run right up to God and look Him innocently in the eyes.

"How lopsided our relationship is, Father," I whispered. "It should have been me."

You're just a child, He answered back. *And I will always do for you what you're helpless to do for yourself.*

No, life is not fair. And for that, I'll be eternally grateful.

9

Second Wind

"Do not call to mind the former things,
Or ponder things of the past.
Behold, I will do something new,
Now it will spring forth;
Will you not be aware of it?
I will even make a roadway in the wilderness,
Rivers in the desert."

—Isaiah 43:18–19 (NASB)

I don't know how or exactly when it happened. I began to notice it first at baby showers.

"Isn't he adorable?" someone would say of the new baby.

"Adorable," I'd agree.

"Isn't that the tiniest little shirt you ever saw?" someone else would ask.

"Hmmm, yes...tiny," I'd say.

Tiny sleepers. Tiny booties. Tiny blankies. And of course, there was always that perfectly tiny baby.

"He has Mike's chin," I told my friend Meagan, when I first held Caleb.

"He has your eyes," I told my friend Stephanie, when I first held Ben.

The truth is, when I'm holding those Calebs and Bens and commenting on chins and eyes, I'm not really thinking of my friends or their husbands. My mouth says all the right things, but my mind is on another child.

I miss my baby. I didn't lose him—he just refused to stay little. If I had seen it coming, I would have fought it. But I didn't, and there it is: I'm annoyed at Zac for being eight.

I suppose you could say I've developed a routine of sorts. After every baby shower, I go home, pore over Zac's baby book, watch an hour or two of his baby videos, and then stand in his bedroom, where I shake my head at week-old apple cores and month-old socks, spiders in jars, and an overall scent of frog.

And I wonder: whatever happened to baby lotion? Did the scent just drift away unnoticed one afternoon? I feel cheated. Someone should have warned me. Someone should've said, "Breathe deeply, this is your last chance." But no one did. And no one warned me of the boy scents to come.

I can't go anywhere without running into memories of my baby. A trip to the grocery store means walking past the baby food aisle. I view pureed peas and creamed carrots with yearning. How I long to buy—just once more—a beautiful, big box of rice cereal.

Even an afternoon in the garden fills my mind with thoughts of Zac. I remember him at two, tottering around behind me while clutching raggedy remnants of a dandelion. "Make wishes, Mama!" he used to urge.

A shopping trip to the mall means walking past the play tugboat where we spent many happy, lazy afternoons together. I slow my steps as I approach and stare jealously at all the mothers lounging on couches that surround the play area. While their little ones clamber about the boat, I remember my own curly-headed boy, who was never content to stay on the deck but had to instead hoist himself onto the railing.

"Look, Mama! I'm not holding onto anything!" I'd stand

nearby, ready to catch him if he missed a step, and play along when he pointed out imaginary "snarks" and other dangers in the depths of the blue carpet. When did he last say "snarks"?

Mourning comes in stages. I'm past denial; for a long while now, I've been stuck in the anger stage. Though I had never minded food thrown on the high chair or floor or me, I'm angry now if Zac leaves water rings on the table. Though I hadn't minded washing diapers, I suddenly have no patience for underwear left on the bathroom floor.

I'm frustrated at how he's changed. He doesn't want advice or help now. He's determined to do things his own way. He does first and thinks later (if at all). It didn't bother me when he was a toddler. I found it endearing. Now, that sort of independence annoys me.

"No need to worry, Mom," he told me one afternoon. The need to worry hit me hard.

"I heard a noise when you were vacuuming. So when you went to answer the phone, I took the vacuum cleaner apart."

"And...?!!

"And I'm sure Dad can put it back together. Anyway, it's not making those weird noises now."

He was wrong about his dad but right about the noises. The vacuum cleaner quit making noises then and there—of any kind. And I didn't find it cute or endearing or tolerable. Just...irritating.

My impatience startles me. I don't like myself this way. Just as I miss the child he once was, I miss the mother I used to be. I long for the nights when I'd whisper as Zac was drifting off to sleep, "I always wanted a boy just like you." These days, I want the boy he used to be.

Before, I was Mary, a mother who watched and pondered and treasured things in my heart. Now I'm Lot's wife, torn between the future and the past. She knew better than to look back at Sodom; she'd been warned. But everything familiar was behind her. Despite the warning, despite her feet walking mechanically and obediently toward the unknown, she took one last, longing look—and in an instant she turned to salt.

My metamorphosis has been painfully slow. I feel each grain and chafe under every layer of salt. And still, I can't stop looking.

In the middle of my musing, I hear Zac "yahooing." I watch through the living room window as he screeches past on his bicycle, one hand on the handlebar and one clutching an almost-eaten popsicle. He rides through my herb bed, crushing the comfrey's tall green stems.

A gust of wind brushes the trees, eliciting another shout from Zac. He bellows at the hens and races around the chicken yard, leaving a flurry of feathers in his wake.

Popsicle gone, he tosses the stick and wrapper over his shoulder and wheels away, perhaps to torment the sheep, perhaps to annihilate more herbs. Another gust of wind sends the forgotten wrapper skittering across the lawn.

"God, help me," I say out loud. I'm almost fully salt now; I can feel it.

Something crashes outside. I head out to investigate.

"What was that?" I ask my husband.

"I don't know—maybe a branch broke off or something." Dave isn't worried.

Zac rides up and slides to a stop.

"Zac, did you hear that loud noise a minute ago?"

He shakes his head.

"Well, it had to be something." I start toward the shed. Behind me, Zac comments, "You know how women are, Dad. Always afraid of something. Noises and bears and stuff."

And boys who grow up when their mothers aren't looking, I add silently.

It's getting worse by the moment. Now he's calling me a "woman." I feel as if he's slipping away, second by precious second, as though before my very eyes he's leaping out of my arms and into the world of men. How did this happen?

I walk, lost in my thoughts, until I reach the shed. There I spot Dave's new weed eater leaning awkwardly against a fence post, the apparent source of the mysterious crash. I reach down and take hold of it, intending to put it away.

"Don't."

I turn around to see Zac standing behind me, watching.

"What?" I ask.

"I don't want you using that, Mom."

I can't quite believe he's speaking to me with such an authoritative tone. For a split second I gather my words into the makings of a lecture, dotted with favorites like "respect" and "impertinence." But he continues.

"That weed eater is way too heavy for you, Mom. I don't want you to get hurt."

Countless times in the past, similar words have made their way from my mouth to his ears.

"Don't play with that, Zac. That will hurt you."

"Hot! Hot! Don't touch, honey—no, no!"

Did he learn concern from me? Or has he soaked in that protectiveness from his father, who opens my doors and carries all things heavy?

He's a miniature version of Dave in that moment. The lecture dissipates. I don't tell Zac I was only moving the weed eater. I don't say anything at all. I simply set it down.

He starts digging around a forgotten patch of garden next to the shed, humming, and announces he's going to make his own garden there. Since he lost my gloves yesterday, he has to dig with bare hands.

I walk a few steps away to the grape arbor, where I sit and watch my man-child. I try to ignore the panic settling around me, but I can feel its fingers clutching at my throat. I feel adrift; aimless and without purpose. I don't know what to do. How can I parent a child I no longer recognize, a child who thinks I'm the one who needs protecting? When did we cross that line?

Minutes pass. He hums; I listen. The wind kicks up again.

"Ouch!" he yelps.

"What happened?"

"Something poked me!" He searches through a pile of weeds and makes a discovery.

"Ohhh…I know what this is."

I wait, fully expecting him to tell me the genus and species, to describe the history of the plant and its particular uses. Nothing would surprise me at that moment.

"Look what poked me, Mom. It's just a baby dandelion that hasn't been born yet!"

The wind whips hard against my face, and I'm sure it's to blame for the sudden tears I feel welling. I thought he was too grown up for dandelions.

He brings me the offending weed as evidence. The hand he holds out is dirt-covered and grass-stained and suddenly much smaller than it has looked in months.

I peer beyond my tears into the green depths of his eight-year-old eyes. The man he will become stares back at me, but I can still see my baby. He's there, too.

I didn't miss it.

I understand, in that second, exactly who my son is. Or rather, who he isn't. He's no longer a baby, but he's not yet a man. Not even a man-child.

And I can see clearly *where* he is, in that one stark moment. He's up again on that railing, straddling two worlds. On one side, there's the safety of his childhood, full of blankies and sleepers and booties and all the rest. On the other side, deep and unfathomable waters.

Just as he did so many years ago, he's attacking this railing like a gymnast on a balance beam. He's twirling and hopping and occasionally dipping one curious toe into the murky, beckoning depths.

"Look, Mom! No hands!"

Someone should hold his hand. Someone should be there to point out snarks and ferocious, unborn dandelions.

You're still needed, God whispers. *He'll always need you*.

As I stand there, holding his dirt-covered little hand and peering into his beautiful, trusting eyes, the wind makes a final blast, scouring the sky and my heart. The annoyance I've carried all these months skitters away, like Zac's forgotten popsicle wrapper; and then…it's gone. Stillness settles both around and within me.

I feel the shift. Lot's wife is gone; not a single grain of salt remains. The wind has done its job well. Where the pillar once stood, the heart of Mary is unearthed.

"Can I tell you something, Zac?"

He nods.

"I always wanted a boy just like you."

10

Refuge

"O God, have pity, for I am trusting you! I will hide beneath the shadow
of your wings until this storm is past. I will cry to the God of heaven who
does such wonders for me. He will send down help from heaven to save
me, because of his love and his faithfulness. He will rescue me."

—Psalm 57:1–3 (TLB)

*F*or as long as I can remember, I've loved storms. Others
may frown at the darkening sky and the boom and crackle of
nearing thunder, but my senses leap to greet the squall. I've
always felt there's something electrifying and wonderful
about the need to take cover.

My sisters feel the same way. Megan, in particular, shares
my anticipation. We take turns at weather patrol. She calls
me with updates. "Did you hear? They've upgraded tomorrow's storm to a gale warning!" You can hear the giddiness
behind her words. She wants it all—swaying trees, downed
power lines, an hour or a day without electricity. I want it
too.

Here in the Pacific Northwest, we are almost guaranteed
one or two good clobberings every fall. On our particular
country road, experience has taught us to prepare for long
stretches without electricity. We've gone as long as four days
before the power company gets around to our little rural

road. So the minute we hear a storm is brewing, I begin my tried-and-true routine: I wash the dishes and finish up the laundry. I pull out extra candles and flashlights. I send Dave to the woodshed to find the kerosene lamp, and when he brings it in, I set it on the kitchen table along with a deck of cards and a board game or two. I start something chunky and delicious: a pot of stew, or chili, or chowder. I make coffee and store it in a thermos. And because we're on a private well, which operates on electricity, I fill every available container with water—and then I wait, impatient for the show to begin.

Sometimes people will overhear Megan and me talking in excited tones about a coming storm and they'll shake their heads at us. "What's the deal?" I've been asked, more than once. I'm not sure how to answer. I don't quite know how to explain my storm-hunger, except to say that it satisfies my need to nest. I think all mothers are the same in that respect. We love mugs of cocoa and fuzzy socks and warm sweaters, because we know that small tummies and cold feet and little skinny, naked arms need those things. And when we get to be the provider, it feels good.

When Zac was little, I started playing a storm game with him. I don't know where it came from. We were sitting side by side on the couch with a book and a blanket, and I said, "Let's pretend we're on a mountain. We've been out taking a walk together—just you and me—and we've been so busy picking berries and watching baby bears wrestle each other that we haven't noticed the black clouds taking over the sky. But there they are. The wind starts blowing [here I made a pathetic "whoosh" sound] and the air grows cold, and before we know what's happening, we're caught in the middle of a fierce blizzard. Wolves howl on the hills above our heads. We hold hands and start walking. We can't see very far ahead, and we don't know where we are. The snow is piling up fast. It's getting darker by the minute, and the wolves are sounding closer and closer. But suddenly, just when we're thinking we'll never find a way out of that blizzard, we come around a corner and see the opening to a cave. We bend down and crawl inside and find that someone has built a fire, and it's waiting just for us…and there's a warm blanket we can share. And a pile of picture books. And cocoa."

Zac thought that was a pretty good game—the first time. He tolerated it fairly well the second and third time, too, but after that I was just plain pushing my luck. After that, whenever I'd start with "Let's pretend we're on a mountain…" he'd cover his eyes in exasperation and say, wearily, "Oh, not the blizzard again."

If I really want to dig deep, I think my love of storms is probably wrapped up in some way with the tornado that flew over our house when I was a nine-year old girl living in Arkansas. I don't mean to give the impression that I was up dancing on the rooftop, taunting the twister to come and get me. I was actually quite frightened. But my stepfather, Roy, had a plan. He brought us all into the center of the house in an odd, square area that became completely enclosed when the kitchen door and three bedroom doors were shut. He pulled the mattresses from our beds and brought those in with us, then closed the four doors and propped the mattresses against them. The wind racing above our heads was so wild and so powerful that I could hear shingles being ripped from the roof. A window from the other side of the house shattered and the lights went off, leaving the five of us sitting in absolute blackness. I was completely terrified—right up until my stepfather reached across and squeezed my hand.

"There's nothing to worry about, baby-doll. We're going to be all right."

That was all he needed to say. His calm words sucked the fear right out of my chest. He was bigger, stronger. He was smart. I was nothing but a Yankee newcomer—and a little one, at that—but Daddy Roy had lived in the south all his life, and he knew a thing or two about tornadoes. I believed him, and I felt safe.

When we have a storm, I get to be that parent. I get to be the one with the calm voice and the reassuring hug. I get to pull out the lantern and a deck of cards and tell my children, "It's going to be all right." When the winds blow, I get the chance to be my children's refuge.

But there was one storm, one night, that dwarfed all the others and renewed my respect for nature—and reminded me that in all the ways that matter, I'm still a child myself.

Megan informed me the storm was coming, if I remember correctly. I clapped my hands and ran through all my getting ready steps—washing, gathering, filling. But the storm didn't come when predicted. I waited and watched, but by bedtime, it still hadn't arrived. Dave and Zac went ahead to bed, but I sat up to watch the eleven o'clock news and hear the latest weather update. Periodically I went out to the porch to see if a breeze had risen yet. By midnight, too tired to wait any longer, I gave up and crawled into bed next to Dave. I was disappointed, because I figured we'd probably sleep through the whole thing. I figured wrong.

I awoke around 1:30 to sounds of splintering and crashing outside our window. Dave and I sat up in tandem. The moon hung overhead like a searchlight, shooting beams through the frenzied branches of the trees and casting a bright white glow upon the grass. Our usually tranquil back yard was alive with frantic shadows and dappled moonlight and chaos.

We pulled on our robes and went to the front door. Already, limbs littered the front yard. Even as we watched, an enormous branch from an oak tree ten feet away groaned and crackled and dropped, hammering the ground.

The wind was an angry she-bear; it shrieked and moaned and lashed against the treetops. It shook the timbers; it slapped and pounded and flailed against the grove, sending an undulation of moonlit green rippling from one end to the other. The trees yielded to the wind's fury. They twisted and trembled. They rocked and strained and bent from side to side. And I stood and stared as if seeing them for the first time, as if noticing for the very first time how all those massive trees surrounded our tiny house.

We weren't safe, and we knew it.

"Let's go," Dave said.

I followed him back through the house. The wind sought us there. It pushed against the glass, retreated, pounded again and again. It howled in frustration and threw branches against the doors, the windows, the roof.

We scrambled into our clothes and grabbed a blanket for Zac. We woke him and wrapped him, and headed out the door. Just as we stepped onto the front porch, we heard— and felt—something large and heavy slamming against the roof on the other side of the house. We didn't investigate and we didn't wait to see what happened next. We just ran.

Dave started the car and turned on the headlights. Limbs lay everywhere—on the lawn, over my garden beds, across the driveway. We backed over a pile of branches and headed away from the house. We didn't get far—just forty yards or so—when we came upon a large alder lying at the end of the road, blocking our escape. There was no way around it, so Dave threw the car in reverse and backed us up the driveway. While Zac and I waited, he ran to his woodshed to get some tools.

I hadn't felt winds as fierce as those since the tornado in Arkansas—nor had I been as frightened. But this time, my parents weren't inches away, making plans for my safety, protecting me. This time, I was part of the decision-making team. And I felt totally overwhelmed.

"Oh, God," I prayed, when I couldn't take the fear any longer. "Please get us out of this nightmare."

Dave ran back to the car and handed me a flashlight. "Shine it up and watch for falling limbs while I cut through the tree," he instructed, as he revved his chainsaw to life.

I did as he told me. I stood beside him and illuminated the wild canopy over our heads. Three or four times I yelled out a warning when smaller branches snapped off overhead and fell in his direction. After a few minutes, he told me not to worry about the little stuff. "Don't stop me unless you see something big coming down."

It seemed to take forever. As Dave sawed, bits of leaves and twigs and branches pelted his back and his head. Behind us, a large evergreen crashed across the top part of our driveway. The wind continued to screech and wail and my heart pounded against my chest. "Help us, Lord," I prayed again.

Dave finally sawed through two sections of the tree and rolled the center piece off to the side of the road. We jumped back in the car and sped as fast as we could, swerving around the larger limbs in our way. Periodically, branches crashed against our roof. I kept praying.

Our only plan, at first, was to get as far away from our house—and our neighborhood—as possible. Our area of town is the most wooded; as you get closer to town, the trees become sparse. But we knew we couldn't just drive all night.

"Let's go to Phil and Stephanie's," Dave suggested. Our friends lived in a nice, safe, treeless area of town. Dave carpooled with Stephanie to the train station in Seattle every Monday morning; she wouldn't be expecting him for another four hours, but we figured she'd forgive us for waking her early.

She was groggy when she opened the front door, but she snapped awake pretty quickly and moved into "hostess-mode." Before long, she had us settled in sleeping bags on her very comfortable living room couches.

Dave and Zac fell asleep almost immediately. I had to smile at their ability to let it all go. I couldn't. I laid in the darkness, staring at the silhouette of Stephanie's fluttering lilac bush through her living room curtains.

We were safe. We'd had to make a run for it, but we were safe.

"Thank You for saving us," I whispered at the ceiling.

I rolled over and tried to make myself sleep. Visions of falling branches kept forcing my eyes open. The sounds of crackling and groaning and pounding were only in my mind now, but I couldn't shake them.

I thought about all the other storms we'd had—storms that had seemed fun. I remembered times Dave would come in with a pile of firewood for the stove, when I'd be waiting with a cup of coffee ready for him and candles lit all over the place. I loved being the comforter and making things cozy for my family. I loved nurturing them. But this storm had been too much. This storm was bigger than me.

But not bigger than Me.

I heard God's heartbeat in the darkness. I listened to His whispers, and I saw the way things were. I was His child, and He had just provided the comforting, the nurturing, the sheltering I needed. He had brought me out of danger and to a place of safety. I saw that all my feelings of nesting came right from Him; that the heart beating in me came first from my Father, and no matter how long I lived, I would always be His little girl. He would always be just inches away, ready to calm my fears and tuck me into His embrace.

I saw that He is my Refuge.

I don't know how long He spoke to me that night. But I do remember the last whisper I heard, just as I was letting go and drifting off to sleep. In the still of the night, I heard something very familiar.

Let's pretend we're on a mountain. We've been out taking a walk together—just you and Me...

Winter

"A time to weep…a time to mourn"

A young pioneer man, full of confidence and ambition, caught the homesteading bug. He heard that northern Canada was the place to be, so he bought a big chunk of land—sight unseen—and convinced his wife to leave her family and everything familiar and follow his dream. With only their infant daughter and the bare essentials, they left New York and began the long walk north to Canada. But winter came early. The snow started like a light, white mist— more dust than snow. But with each passing mile, the snow's substance and seriousness grew.

Traveling had been hard on the baby, and the cold didn't help matters. She became feverish. She began to cough incessantly. The young mother tried to bundle her tighter, but the snow and wind found openings and burrowed without mercy.

When all seemed hopeless, the couple stumbled on a humble-looking cabin deep in the woods, occupied by an elderly couple, who took the travelers in, fed them, and warmed them the best they could. They stayed two days, resting, but the baby did not improve. On the third day, the elderly couple urged the baby's father to go and fetch the doctor, who lived some eight miles farther into the squall. He agreed, kissed his family goodbye, and started off on his mission.

He didn't come back when he should have. His wife

paced and prayed until she couldn't bear the uncertainty another minute longer. Finally, with the older man at her side to guide her, she set off after her husband.

The snow was waist deep, but they plowed through the drifts. About two miles from the cabin, they spotted the young man standing in the center of a vast, white meadow. He stood perfectly still, gazing back at them and watching their approach. The wife was overjoyed. She called out to him—but her husband didn't respond. Still struggling in the deep snow, she tried to move faster. It seemed to take forever, but she finally crossed the distance between them. When she was close enough to touch him, she lunged forward to take his hand. She meant to tell him how worried she had been when he didn't return, to express how relieved she was to have found him, but the words died on her lips. By the icy touch of his hand and the steady gaze of his unseeing eyes, the woman realized her husband was gone. He had frozen to death in the storm.

Winter can overtake you in a second. One minute, you're strolling through a fertile field, cloaked in warmth and full of hope, and in the next breath your world is transformed. The skies darken, grief falls like ice, and barrenness steals across the landscape and settles upon your heart. The world is stilled, and you find yourself paralyzed by circumstances you never saw coming.

If that's where you find yourself right now, if pain or grief has halted you in your tracks and you see no hope in sight, know this: there's no winter so deep that spring can't reach it eventually. Know also that you're not in that frozen wasteland alone. God is there. He's as near as He's always been—and He still has a plan for your life. He is still at work.

C.S. Lewis said that pain is God's megaphone to the world. That may be true. That may be the only way a deaf world even begins to hear the voice of God. But we're not the world. We're His beloved daughters and sons, and He promises that when our hearts are shattered, He'll be close by. In the stillness of winter, when our souls are hushed and the noise of life has been silenced, all He needs to do is whisper.

Let His breath warm you—and hear His words of comfort.

I see the end from the beginning.
I know your future.
I see around all your corners, and I know the plans I have for you.
I am your hope…and your balm.
I am your healing.

11

Still, Small Voices

"For You formed my inward parts;
You wove me in my mother's womb.
I will give thanks to You, for I am fearfully and wonderfully made;
Wonderful are Your works,
And my soul knows it very well.
My frame was not hidden from You,
When I was made in secret."

—Psalm 139:13–15 (NASB)

Are there more bugs up here?" Zac asked as we stepped onto the escalator at the Oregon Museum of Science and Industry. I secretly hoped not. I'd seen just about all the insects I cared to in the exhibit downstairs.

"I'm not sure."

He wriggled and jiggled tirelessly as we rode upwards. Two hours of exploring had done very little to deplete his energy level. I mused at the injustice. Children have all the energy, but mothers are the ones who really need it. I could use a bit more bounce, if only to keep up with him.

My ponderings ended along with the escalator ride. As always, Zac was full of suggestions about what we should look at next.

"Look, Mom—a fake brain! No—let's look at that big computer thing over there!"

We touched the fake brain. We punched buttons on the big computer thing. We poked and prodded and explored. Just as I was mentally wrapping up the day, ready to point out that we had seen absolutely everything there was to see and it was time to saddle up and head for home, I spotted a sign in front of a curved, black wall.

"The embryos and fetuses in this exhibit show the development of humans before birth. To the best of our knowledge, the survival of these specimens was prevented by natural causes or accidents. These restored specimens are over 25 years old."

That didn't sound good. I hesitated, not at all sure I wanted to see what was on the other side of the wall. But Zac darted into the exhibit, making the decision for us both. I followed.

We entered a dim, gray-carpeted room. Its shape was spherical. Its parameters were defined by the large display wall that curved around in a nearly completed circle, effectively muffling the light and noise outside. Black, spider-like scaffolding crisscrossed the space above our heads, and beyond that, black paint covered the high ceiling. Three dozen or so brightly-lit Plexiglas boxes hung suspended at eye level against the curved wall.

We stopped in front of the first box. It contained a tiny embryo, not quite fully formed but still obviously an embryo. A placard in front of the box announced that "the specimen" had been preserved at twenty-eight days old.

As we walked along the wall and read each card, it became clear that each succeeding embryo was a few days older, a few days more defined than the one before. The third box told us that at fifty-one days, small black dots marked the beginning of a baby's eyes. Leaning close, I could just make out the black dots.

We moved slowly. Zac contented himself with looking,

but I read the description on each sign and scrutinized each fetus.

"55 Days Old: By now the foundation—the organs—are in place. Every organ that's in you is in this tiny embryo."

It seemed impossible. I looked closer, trying to imagine how that small shape could hold all the necessary organs.

"57 Days Old: Fingernails appear on the fingertips. Can you see the soft ribs?" I could.

"11 Weeks Old: The mouth is ready for the thumb."

I must confess, at first my interest was purely scientific. Over the years I had read a number of books about developing life and had seen all those dramatic pictures of unborn babies. Curiosity kept my feet moving, at first. But these were not mere photographs. These were actual, three dimensional forms.

Somewhere along that wall, my attitude changed.

A young pregnant woman walked in with two small girls at her side. My guess was that she was late in her eighth month of pregnancy. With the girls dancing along beside her, she approached the first box and read the placard silently.

I watched her, wondering how she would react.

She made her way quickly to where I stood and then moved around me, heading down to where the fetuses were bigger and more developed. I didn't want her to go to that end of the wall. I had to stop myself from stopping her. As I watched her eyes moving from one baby to the next, I worried for the woman. Just weeks, or maybe days from giving birth, what must she be thinking as she looked inside these boxes? Would the sight of all these miscarried babies make her fear for her own unborn child?

"I am absolutely starving," she announced, kicking my concern right over the wall. "How about you girls? Should we go grab a burger?"

"Yeah!" the girls said in unison. The trio strode out,

chattering happily—and leaving me staring after them in confusion.

Another woman drifted in with a seven- or eight-year old boy. "Oh, look! That's what you were like when you were in my tummy." She laughed. "Aren't they just teeny little things?"

Her son tossed a bored glance at the unmoving shapes. He fiddled with the zipper on his jacket, up and down, up and down. The metal zinged rhythmically. After a dozen zings, he lost interest and tossed his head back.

"C'mon, Mom. I wanna go buy a space model."

"Just one sec," she answered. She walked to the next box, scanned the card, and chuckled. "Amazing. Just amazing." She turned to her son. "Don't you think this is amazing, kiddo?"

Her son kicked at the wall. "I think it's stupid."

She sighed. "Okay. Let's go to the science store."

Only a few minutes after coming into the display, they were gone.

Their nonchalance felt like a slap. I couldn't find words to explain why it bothered me so. I only knew it was wrong.

Zac slipped his hand in mine. "Mom," he asked, "what creatures were these going to be?"

"What?"

"If all these things were alive, what creatures would they be?"

I studied Zac's expression. He wasn't trying to be funny. I could tell he was sincere. His question perplexed me, because it seemed so obvious what they were, especially as we made our way down to the older fetuses. Maybe he couldn't bring himself to see them for what they really were.

"Babies, honey." I whispered. "These are all babies."

His hand felt warm, and very small. It was much smaller than my own, but so very much larger than the hands I saw behind the Plexiglas.

101

One little hand was curved in a tight fist. One hand rested on a baby's cheek. One hand cupped a baby's nose, its thumb still in the child's mouth.

One baby had a long gash on his left leg, quickly sewn together with imprecise stitches. The sight jolted me. Zac had cut his leg in exactly the same place one warm summer day, jumping on a friend's trampoline.

I saw grimaces, smiles, brown hair and red. Each little face was different. Each was lovely, in the way that all babies are lovely.

My eyes misted and all the bright noise and happy confusion on the other side of the wall faded away.

I wanted to stop looking, I really did. I wanted to stop, but I couldn't. It was no longer scientific curiosity that kept me walking along that wall. My compulsion was suddenly of a much different nature. It occurred to me that if the sign outside were to be believed and these babies had all been miscarried, then there were families somewhere in the world who had wanted these children, had waited for these children, and then had grieved for these children. Out of respect for those families, if for no other reason, I felt a strong and sudden need to take a moment at each display and acknowledge the individuality of each unborn child.

The sign had stated that the display was over twenty-five years old. Twenty-five years. If these children had lived, they would be having children of their own by now. This tiny sampling of God's incredible creativity, in these three-dozen faces, made me wonder what loveliness the world had missed.

"They're beautiful, Lord," I breathed. "And You are amazing."

My heart hurt to see such silent, unmoving beauty, and to think that they would be forever nameless.

They're not nameless, my heart heard God saying. *I've held each child—and I've named them all.*

"Can we go, Mom—please?"

I glanced down at my son, who glanced back up with beautiful, pleading eyes. He tugged at me with little boy hands while youthful energy wriggled through his skinny legs.

As we left the circle of babies, Zac ran his hand along the black wall, leaving a trail of small fingerprints. I stifled my urge to tell him not to touch the pristine surface.

No, I decided. There should be a sign of life here.

12

Rachel Rose

"When I thought how to understand this, it was too painful for me."
—Psalm 73:16 (NKJV)

I'm going to court today. After a few hours of writing, I'll turn off my laptop, grab my keys and my purse, and head into town to pick up my friend Denise. I'll ask her if she's hungry. Sometimes, if she's feeling up to it, we'll stop for a quick bite on our way to the county courthouse. More often than not, she can't eat.

I've lost count of how many trips we've made together. Thirty or more, I figure. In the beginning, we cried so hard my head would hurt for hours afterwards. We still cry—and we do so often—but it sneaks up on us now. Sometimes, without any warning at all, the truth will crash upon us like some massive, merciless wave. It tosses disbelief to the side and grabs our shoulders and shakes our eyes wide open, forcing us to see the truth: Rachel is gone.

There are eight defendants in this murder case. Four of the men have pled guilty already; four others deny they had any part in the brutal act. Two trials are scheduled in the coming months. Two men will likely face the death penalty.

All those numbers mean nothing to us, really. They don't sink in the way others do. Denise keeps meticulous track of the truly important numbers on a calendar hanging on her bedroom wall—the calendar her eyes seek out first thing each morning after she wakes from another fitful night. "Rachel gone three months," it said on December 23rd last year. "Rachel's 19th birthday," she wrote in one of January's boxes. Last week, I saw the pocket calendar she keeps in her purse. "Rachel in heaven one year," she wrote in September. Those dates are the only numbers that matter anymore.

Rachel was not my daughter, but I loved her. And though my winter cannot compare to the one that has overtaken Denise, I still feel its frigid fingers squeezing my heart. I still wake sometimes in the night, hurting and missing her. I think about her startling, ice blue eyes and the way she saw straight to your soul whenever those eyes settled upon you. I remember the way her smile warmed you down to your toes and made strangers wish they knew her.

Alarm trickled in slowly in that first week. Denise was the first to believe something was wrong when Rachel didn't return to her dad's, where she'd been living. She called us, she called Rachel's friends, she called the police. "Rachel's missing," she said. We all told her not to worry. We said Rachel would turn up. "She's eighteen," we reminded Denise, as if that explained her disappearance.

"It's not like her," she answered back.

We didn't know what to think. Rachel had been our prodigal, the girl we worried about and prayed for. She had gone from a giggly fifteen-year-old who cried at her own baptism and chided her older sister, Meghan, for staying out too late—to being a giggly seventeen- and eighteen-year-old who stopped coming to church and started trusting the wrong people. Sometimes she didn't return to her father's until the late hours of the night and early morning. But things had changed in recent weeks. Our prodigal had turned back for home. Only twelve days before her disappearance, she came to our September 11th prayer service with her mom. She joined one of the small groups and took her turn praying for our nation and for the family members of those lost on September 11, 2001. She told her former youth leader, Corey, that something had changed in her life and that Jesus had never been more real to her than He was at that moment. She hugged me before she left, and said she'd like to come clean the bathrooms of our new church building. "I don't care what I do—I just want to come and help," she said, laughing.

And before she stepped out of the church, she turned and flashed her famous smile at my husband. He smiled back, and waved, but she didn't break her gaze. She just kept smiling at him and staring, almost as if she knew she was saying goodbye. It was the last time we saw her.

Denise was the last to speak with her. They were both in their cars, both on their cell phones that Monday night. They chit-chatted about trivial things, and then Rachel asked, "Is there anything going on at church tonight that we could go to?" Denise suggested they wait until the next night and come to our women's Bible study together. Rachel agreed. Then Denise's reception started to fade. "I'm going through a drive-through. I'll have to call you back," she said. But when she tried again later, there was no answer.

What we didn't know then—and wouldn't know until much later, when it all came to light in a taped confession— was that Rachel was kidnapped just a short time after that conversation. Some new friends lured her to a duplex, where her ex-boyfriend was waiting. Standing just 4'11" and weighing a slight 98 pounds, Rachel was no match for even the smallest of the men that surrounded her. We have no clear motive other than jealousy—we may never know the true motive—but for whatever unimaginable reason they decided to do so, these men beat Rachel, bound and gagged her, and shoved her inside a large black duffel bag. When the woman who owned the duplex came home and saw what was happening, she didn't help Rachel and she didn't call the police. Instead, she told her boyfriend and the others to get "it" out of her house.

So they did. They took Rachel—still in the duffel bag—and threw her into the back of a jeep. They drove her out to a remote gravel pit in the Cascade Mountain foothills, some thirty miles from her home, and dug a shallow grave while she waited, knowing she would die. They then pulled her out of the bag, forced her to disrobe, made her lie face down in her grave—and shot her to death.

While this was happening, her mother was home finishing her take-out dinner. Her father, Bill, was at his house watching the evening news. Her sister Meghan was busy tending to her beautiful eighteen-month old daughter, Jaida. My husband and I were at a conference, standing in a room full of pastors and their wives, worshiping. While Rachel drew her last breath, our hearts kept beating. Our lived ticked on.

Denise knew first. She hadn't yet convinced us, or the police or the media. She couldn't make any of us else feel what she felt—that her daughter was no longer living. But she knew.

"Rachel's dead," she told Dave on Thursday.

He tried to soften her words, to backtrack for her. He tried to create scenarios in which Rachel was just off somewhere ignoring our repeated calls to her cell phone. But Denise stopped him.

"You don't understand," she said. "I know she's gone. I feel it."

Meghan knew it too. She was closer to Rachel than to anyone else on earth, closer than most sisters will ever be. When Rachel's heart stopped beating, Meghan's heart responded.

"I can feel it too," she told her mother.

I left that Sunday for a five-day trip to southern California. My destination was Murrieta, specifically, the annual

Calvary Chapel Pastors' Wives' Conference held at our conference center there. The grounds are peaceful, beautiful, and serene. The times I'd spent there in the past had always been times of heart- and soul-mending. But I could not enter into the rest I came seeking. I could not clear my mind of Rachel.

I phoned home for updates several times a day. "Flyers have been posted up and down the I-5 corridor," I heard on one call. On another, I learned that the police had finally taken Rachel's disappearance seriously and the media frenzy had begun.

Then on Tuesday afternoon, I heard news that made my throat tighten and my stomach lurch. "They found her car," my husband told me. It contained Rachel's Bible and some index cards with Scripture verses written upon them, but little else.

By Tuesday night, I felt it too. I sat outside next to a lake surrounded by lighted palm trees, and let my grief pour out of me. Two friends sat on either side, crying with me and praying.

On Friday morning, with a restless heart and several empty hours before my flight home, I was driving toward Huntington Beach to walk the pier and watch the surfers when my cell phone rang.

"They've found her body," Dave said. "Rachel is with the Lord."

I don't remember parking my rental car or walking the length of the pier. I don't recall reaching the end of the dock and walking around Ruby's Diner. But I remember the view that met my eyes when I finally reached my destination and leaned over the pier's railing. I can still see the sheen and color of the sea below, black and glassy, sparkling in the sunlight like an endless field of just-polished obsidian.

I stared at the vastness of the ocean, stretching in an unbroken, unending line, and remembered a bedtime talk of long ago.

"What does 'eternity' mean, Mom?" Zac asked.

God gave me an answer to share, something that helped us both grasp the enormity of forever.

"If we caught one of your teardrops in a little jar, and then we got in a boat and went out to the very center of the ocean—so far out we couldn't see a speck of land anymore—and we poured your tear over the side, do you think you could ever find it again?"

He shook his head no.

"Would you even want to?"

He shook his head again.

"Life is just a teardrop, Zac. Eternity is the ocean. When you're in heaven with the Lord, you won't miss your life. You won't even think about it again—and you'll never reach the end of eternity."

It had been one thing to speak of heaven with my four-year-old, safe in the belief that his life would be long and full. It was completely another matter to place Rachel in the center of forever.

"She was so young, Father," I prayed beneath my breath. "She was too young. She had her whole life ahead of her. And she was happy."

I closed my eyes and saw Rachel gliding into a room, lighting it up with only her presence. I saw her dancing, and smiling, and laughing.

"Oh, Lord, You know she was always so happy."

His whisper came quickly.

She's happy still. Right now, right this moment, Rachel is more joyful, more delighted than you've ever seen her.

"But why did You permit this to happen? Oh, Father, she was our prodigal. She wanted her life to change. She was ready. She wanted to turn around—and she was doing so. Rachel was headed back."

She is My prodigal—and I've brought her all the way home.

I wanted to take the comfort His whispers offered. But I

wasn't yet ready. I'd formed a list in my mind, a list of every-thing that had changed in the span of a single heartbeat.

In a heartbeat, Rachel was betrayed.

She was discarded.

She lost her future.

In a heartbeat, she was ripped from us.

But my Father had His own list, and as I stood staring at the vastness of the ocean, He whispered these words to my heart.

In a heartbeat, I took My daughter home.

I held her.

I looked in her eyes.

I brought My prodigal to the feast.

In a heartbeat, I filled her emptiness and healed My loved one of every wound.

I heard, and let His words begin to soothe the raw places of my heart. The truth of what He said didn't keep me from grieving, but what I learned there on that pier kept me from wishing Rachel back with us. Her reality is joy. How could I not want that for her? From that moment till now, regardless of the tears and the persistent ache, I've never once wished I could change things for Rachel. I wish I could change them for the rest of us. Now, when I wake in the night missing her, I ask for only one thing: I ask for God to come quickly. After all, Rachel is where we all want to be.

So I'm going to court today. When I get to Denise's apart-ment, she won't quite be ready. I'll sit on the edge of her bed and talk to her while she brushes her hair and puts on her lipstick. And, like I do every time, I'll look first at the pictures of Rachel on her wall and nightstand. I'll look at the calen-dar with all those important numbers written and circled. I'll look for a long moment at the small square of paper Denise taped to her mirror the day after Rachel's body was found— the one on which she wrote,

"Every day for You, Jesus,
I can live every day for You."

And for the hundredth time, I'll be in awe of God's sustaining power, in awe of the fact that in the darkest, bleakest winter of her life, my friend keeps worshiping God...and keeps waiting for spring.

What a comfort to know it's just a heartbeat away.

13

The Privilege

"I consider everything a loss compared to the surpassing greatness of knowing Christ Jesus my Lord, for whose sake I have lost all things....I want to know Christ and the power of his resurrection and the fellowship of sharing in his sufferings."

—Philippians 3:8, 10

Tamera's black corkscrew curls bounce and swing as she struts toward the adults around the table. No one in the world walks the way this child does. I adore her, and she knows it. She catches my eye and favors me with a grin, then makes her "sniffer face": she scrunches up her eyes and wrinkles her nose, then snorts in and out, in and out. I could watch her do it all day. She knows that too.

She stops prancing only long enough to make one precarious twirl. She manages to keep from falling over, laughs at herself, and takes a quick slurp from her sippy cup. She spies my purse, picks it up, and begins to inspect the contents. Finding my cell phone, she squeals and holds it to her ear. Clearly, she's been watching her mom on the phone. "Uh huh," she says. That's about the only discernible phrase. The rest is a rush of syllables, interjected with giggles and gasps. She's having a conversation with the most fascinating person in the room: herself.

My youngest sister, Tarri, tosses ice in two glasses and

opens two cans of soda. She pours slowly, then sets the glasses down in front of her guests. Mark and Jane have driven twenty hours to sit here in Tarri's kitchen. We didn't want them to come—we prayed that they wouldn't—but now that they're here, we can't help but like them.

My brother-in-law, Todd, walks through the kitchen and takes a plate of hamburger patties out of the fridge. I can see his strategy: focus on the barbecue and not on the strangers at his table. I hope it works for him, but I doubt it.

"Dah!" Tamera shrieks when she spots him. Todd pulls a drawer open and grabs a spatula.

"Dah!"

"What, baby?" Todd asks.

She makes her sniffer face for him and waits for a response.

"You're funny," Todd says, but he's not smiling.

Tamera moseys over and hands me the phone. We all turn to stare at her.

"Isn't she beautiful?" I can't help but ask. Mark and Jane nod. My other sister, Megan, nods too. Tarri wipes the counter but doesn't say anything.

In a few days, these people will turn their van around and head back to South Dakota. They'll take Tamera with them—our Tamera. The girl my sister and brother-in-law call daughter. The girl Megan and I call niece. Because she's half Native American, we knew from the beginning that this day might come. We knew she may be taken from us, but the thought was too hurtful to face. Now we have no choice.

Todd and Tarri tried everything possible to adopt her. They made calls and wrote letters. They appealed to Tamera's grandmother to intervene. They went before a Tribal Council and begged. Mostly, they prayed. In the end, that's really all they had left.

In one sense, God answered their prayers. Mark and Jane are Christians. Their faith is brand new, but it's genuine.

They can't stop talking about Jesus and their fellowship back home and what their new faith means to them. I'm relieved. But I'm also hurting. I know Tarri's anguish intimately. I know exactly what emotions she's suffering, because I've been the foster mother in this story before.

My baby was also brown-skinned and beautiful. The first time I held Isidro, I stared down into eyes so dark they appeared black, eyes that seemed too large for the face of a two-month-old baby. When he turned his gaze from the social worker to me, he was so beautiful it made my heart ache. I think a part of me knew right then that I would some-day grieve over him.

It was a snowy afternoon, two days before Christmas, when I drove to a neighboring town to pick him up. Isidro's caseworker had phoned us in desperation. She'd called every foster family in her district, but no one was willing to take him. As she put it, "No one wants to be bothered with a baby at Christmas." I couldn't help but note the irony of her statement.

"I have a feeling you're going to have him for a while," she warned, as though that would be an unpleasant thing. I felt a surge of hope at her words. "Mom traded his crib and baby formula for drugs, so we don't expect her to come back for him any time soon."

I looked down at his solemn little face and brushed my finger against his silky cheek. "Let's go home, baby," I said.

It had been ten years since I'd last heard an infant's cry in the middle of the night. Those ten years showed in my energy level, but I still loved holding him in the dark, listening to his little drinking noises. I loved the warmth of him, the smell of his skin, the touch of his hands on my face as he explored my eyes, my mouth.

I didn't think of Isidro as my foster baby. He was just my baby. It didn't take long for him to feel the same. Within a week, he recognized my voice and would turn toward me when I walked into the room.

I heard him fussing in the nursery at church one Sunday and went in to investigate.

"Here she is, little guy," the nursery worker said. She walked him over to me and I took him in my arms. He calmed down instantly, looked up in my face, and smiled his first smile—confirming what I already knew: I was his mother. He knew it too.

Dave worried, rightly, that I was too attached. He loved Isidro, but he had an instinct that cautioned him against leaving his heart open. I had no such instinct. My only impulse was to pull him closer.

I wasn't ready when a new social worker called. "We've found relatives who want to take the baby," was how he began our conversation. I nearly dropped the phone. It took three more weeks to work through the details. The new mother was a distant cousin; she and her husband had been married seven years and couldn't conceive. They had only recently moved from Mexico and couldn't speak English, either. I wanted to interview them, to find out if they knew not to microwave his formula, to see if they were the kind of people who would be patient in the dark when their bodies ached for bed, to ask them why they were doing this to me; but of course the social worker knew better than to arrange such a meeting.

On the day he came to take Isidro, dusky blue hyacinths and yellow daffodils appeared in my garden. Winter fled— from everywhere except my heart.

Dave opened the door and greeted the caseworker. They both looked at me apologetically, waiting for a word.

"I'll get him."

He was still asleep when I looked in the crib. His hand

rested flat against the green and white flannel sheet. I touched his skin briefly, lightly, and listened to the slow and even, in and out of his sweet breathing.

I meant to wrap him in his softest blanket, the checkered fleece one I bought for him the day he came home. But when I tugged it off the side of his crib and held it in my arms, I couldn't let it go. Instead, I drew it to my face and took in the deepest breath I could hold. Isidro was there, in that scent. They'd give him other blankets, but I needed the one that smelled like him. I needed it more than he did. I folded it in a small square, walked over to my bed, and hid it under my pillow.

I went back to the crib and watched him sleeping for another minute, then reached in and laid my hand against his back. I traced soft circles between his little shoulders and along his spine. He stirred and drew in a deep, slow breath.

I wrapped him in his blue and green elephant blanket and picked him up for the last time. His breath was warm and soft against my neck, his black hair like silk against my chin. I meant to talk to him, to pour sounds of comfort in his ear and fill his mind with the memory of my voice. I had a long list of things I wanted to say. I wanted mostly to tell him that I loved him, and that no matter what else happened in his life, I would be somewhere in the world still loving him. I wanted him to know a part of him would stay with me forever and a part of me would go with him on his journey. But none of those words found a way past the ice that had crept from my heart to my throat. I couldn't speak, and I couldn't pray. I just stood and rocked my baby, while streaks of sunlight pierced the darkness of the room and birds sang outside my window.

I didn't walk him to the social worker's car. Instead, I bent down and tucked him carefully into his car seat and stared into his dark, beautiful eyes one final time. He kicked his legs against the blanket and smiled up at me, and I wondered if he wondered where we were going. I stood alone at the window and watched as Dave walked them both down our porch steps. I didn't cry until I could no longer see the taillights of the car, not until the sound of tires on our gravel had faded to silence. But once I started, I couldn't stop.

I cried when Dave took Isidro's crib apart to return to the friends who had loaned it to us. I cried the next morning when I woke at seven and realized I had slept through the night. I sat on the floor and sobbed when I swept the laundry room one morning and the corner of the broom pulled a small blue bootie out from under the washing machine. And when the scent of spring rushed through an open window one afternoon and caught me by surprise, I collapsed against the kitchen counter and cried and cried and cried— because I didn't want life to continue on as if nothing had happened.

When I wasn't crying, I prayed. I prayed that they'd bring him back. I prayed the other couple would miss their simpler life and return Isidro to where he belonged. I prayed and I waited for God to fix this mistake.

Almost a month after he was taken, I was sitting in church on a Wednesday night listening to two of our missionaries to Russia. Chris and Katherine Knox told us stories about the church they'd planted in Perm and the people who listened hungrily to the gospel presentation during street outreaches. I was glad for the new souls in the kingdom, but I only half listened to their words. My head was full of Isidro.

After the presentation, Tarri and I went up to talk with Chris and look at pictures of the Russian people and the new church. Tarri's interest was genuine, but my smile and my questions were simply polite.

Chris pointed out the faces one by one and told us the life stories behind each. He talked about the schools and how open they were to Americans. He told us of the children

117

who clamored about their legs, wanting nothing more than a little attention from the strangers. Then he began to describe the orphanages they'd visited. He began to paint a picture of babies in need—babies who needed clean clothes and food and loving arms. Babies who needed mothers. The more he talked, the more desperate I felt, and the more my heart ached.

But then he said something that cut straight through my pain. He'd been telling us about a ten-year old girl whose mother had abandoned her on the side of the road. Katherine heard about the girl and went to meet her. In short time, she fell in love with the child, and even though she was single at the time, she decided to adopt the little girl. She went to work with a fury, making phone calls and meeting in person with anyone who had any kind of authority over the child. Every effort she made seemed to fail, but she didn't quit. She persisted, week after week after week, even when doors kept shutting in her face and every answer she heard was "no." Finally, the Lord spoke to her and put an end to her struggle. Chris told it this way:

"She just kept grieving over that little girl and trying to figure a way to make it work out the way she wanted. But then one day, in the middle of her fretting, God spoke to her. He said, 'Katherine, if I'm not in this thing, you need to die to it.'"

I stood there at the front of the church staring at Chris and hearing his words ringing in my mind. Though he said, "Katherine," what I heard instead was a whisper for me.

Shannon, if I'm not in this thing, you need to die to it.

Without a word, I turned and walked out the church door. I didn't stop walking until I'd reached the edge of our church property. Stars were beginning to appear on the gray canvas over my head, but I wasn't admiring the view. I wasn't conscious of much of anything except the awful challenge God had just placed before me.

I lifted my eyes and drew a ragged breath. "How am I supposed to do that, Lord? How do I die to my need for Isidro?"

Trust that I have done this thing.

I recoiled.

Oh, God, please let me believe anything but that. Let me believe You were just off dealing with somebody else when they came to get my baby. Let me believe You were distracted at that moment and You simply didn't notice when they sliced my heart in two.

But He reminded me of His sovereignty.

You know the truth. You know My eyes never leave you. I was there, daughter, and I noticed. More than that, I allowed this pain.

"But why, Lord? Why would You do this?" I asked, struggling to accept the truth. "Why would You let me hurt this way?"

I searched the sky, and waited. And then He whispered again.

This is the fellowship of My suffering.

This? This loss, this overwhelming sadness, was what that Scripture meant? I began to argue. "Lord, this isn't the same thing at all. You suffered differently. You were betrayed, beaten, misunderstood, rejected. This is completely different. This is me wanting someone I can't have."

But even as the argument was forming in my mind, His answer came with it.

"O Jerusalem, Jerusalem...How often I wanted to gather your children together, as a hen gathers her chicks under her wings, but you were not willing!"

I saw the truth. He *did* know what it was to love someone from afar. He knew what it was to have a longing to hold someone you couldn't.

He knew what it was to lose a Child.

God knew my heartache. And now I knew His.

What I didn't yet know was how often I'd need to share the comfort He'd given me.

※

It's Sunday. Mark and Jane have come with us to church today. I thought it very brave of them, because they know our entire church is grieving. They know they're the reason for the red eyes they see on all these faces. We walk by their side to give them strength. We introduce them. And at the very end of the service, Dave calls them forward to stand in front of our church family along with Todd and Tarri, their boys Christian and Nathan, and Tamera.

He prays for them all. He reminds them—and us—that God is in control. He praises God for His sovereignty and asks for a healing touch on our wounded hearts.

The only person untouched by sadness is Tamera. She dances and prances, she twirls and laughs and gasps and smiles. She comes to me for a hug, and when it seems that no one is looking, I pull a pair of scissors from my purse and clip a long black coil from her hair. I'm the last to get one. Tarri's curl is in a small silver box on top of her dresser. Megan has one, too. I put my piece in my coin purse and kiss Tamera's cheek.

We stand outside and stall for almost an hour, talking with Mark and Jane about the route they'll take back to South Dakota. Talking about their van, and the kind of gas mileage they're getting. Talking about the marshmallow clouds drifting over our heads.

And when there's nothing more we can say, Tarri walks Tamera over to the van and places her carefully in her car seat. She kisses her, and whispers something I can't hear in Tamera's ear. She slides the door shut slowly and backs away. She smiles and waves at Tamera's silhouette, but the tears have already begun streaming down her face. Todd pulls her into his arms.

As the van leaves the church parking lot, sounds of mourning fill the air. We gather around Todd and Tarri. Arms are everywhere, touching, clutching, comforting. Megan holds Tarri from one side, I hold her from the other. Tarri's voice is but a whisper; she barely speaks, but I hear her question through her tears.

"Will she remember me?"

I tell her yes. It's only the beginning of what she needs to hear and what I want to say, but I'll have to wait for all the rest. When she's ready, there's more.

I want to tell my sister that she will always be Tamera's mother, just as I will always be Isidro's. That she will search for Tamera's face in heaven, as I will search for the dark, beautiful eyes I miss so much. That nothing she did for Tamera has been in vain, nothing has been lost. Every brush of her hand against Tamera's face, every gentle hug and tender word, every loving moment she and Todd created will linger in Tamera's life.

I'd like to tell her that it's a privilege to make your arms a safe harbor, if only for a moment, and that I believe the love we give a child somehow becomes a part of them. It burrows into their cells and strengthens their bones. It changes them—forever.

And I want to tell her that through this pain she'll understand God's heart in a way she couldn't otherwise. I want to tell her it is an honor to share in the fellowship of His suffering.

But her Father wants to tell her that Himself.

14

Simeon's Gift

"Simeon was there and took the child in his arms, praising God. 'Lord,' he said, 'now I can die content! For I have seen him as you promised me I would. I have seen the Savior you have given to the world.'"
—Luke 2:28–29 (TLB)

"Do you want to hold my baby?" she asks.

I look down at the girl I love so much, lying on a hospital bed. Diana's eyes are red-rimmed, her face pale. She sniffles and holds the still blue bundle out to me.

Do I want to hold her baby?

Every part of me wants to say no.

Only three months earlier, Scott and Diana showed up on our doorstep early one morning, visibly upset and asking for prayer. We let them talk, and heard news that broke our hearts. Diana had seen her obstetrician the day before. After doing tests on Diana's baby, he had given them a devastating diagnosis. Their unborn son had a condition called *arthorgryposis*. The fact that he had it in such an early stage of pregnancy meant it was severe. His tiny arms and legs didn't move. The first ultrasound technician to notice his stillness had hit Diana's stomach over and over, trying to force the baby to react. Unless God intervened, the baby would die—probably before he was born.

Death terrified Diana. She'd never known anyone to die. She had an overwhelming fear of heaven, though we tried to calm her, tried to convince her that she could trust what Jesus said about the place He went to prepare for us. I asked her once what she was most afraid of.

"I'm most afraid that I won't be with Scott and the kids. I'm afraid I'll get there and I won't be able to find them. Or that I'll get there first and I'll be all alone."

We couldn't change her mind. She simply would not be comforted. When we studied the Book of Revelation in our women's Bible study, her fear intensified. She used to run home the moment I finished teaching, afraid the rapture might happen while she was away and she'd be forever separated from her family.

I prayed God would heal Diana of her fear, but I also thanked Him for the courage she'd shown in so many other areas of life. When she and Scott were teenagers, and not yet married, she became pregnant. Diana already had a relationship with God, and because she knew it was the right thing to do, she carried her baby to term, kissed him goodbye, and gave him up for adoption.

I had seen Diana's pain in unguarded moments when something occurred that brought her firstborn to mind. Britton's adoptive parents—a youth pastor and his wife—sent regular letters and photographs. Diana displayed them prominently on her refrigerator next to those of Madison and Gabriel, the girl and boy God blessed them with after she and Scott were married. She knew she had made the right decision, but she'd been left with a hole in her heart, nonetheless.

And now there'd be a new hole.

"Haven't we hurt enough?" Diana cried, when they brought the news to us. "Why do we have to suffer another loss? Why does this baby have to die?"

We didn't have any answers for them. All we could do was listen and pray.

Our church family rallied around them. Nicole watched Madison and Gabriel when Diana had doctor's visits. Mary Ann kept the prayer chain up-to-date. Cindy brought meals. Tarri and I took turns driving her to Seattle for ultrasound appointments.

The first time I saw the unmoving form of that tiny baby on the screen, I fell apart. I'd watched other ultrasounds and I knew those little arms and legs should be moving around, swimming, reaching. But he was still. Except for a strong, steady heartbeat, Diana's baby was perfectly still. The full weight of sadness fell upon me. I sobbed while Diana held my hand in a firm grasp. I had come there to be a comfort for her, but for a moment, she had to be my rock.

Diana's baby was a curiosity to the hospital staff. During her visits, interns and technicians would often crowd the room.

"This condition is rare," one explained to her. "We only see an average of four such cases a year in the entire Pacific Northwest."

Others suggested she and Scott donate the baby's remains for scientific study. This suggestion was given while she still carried the baby, while we were all still praying for a miracle.

"You really should consider termination," the doctor said during their very first consultation—and the next one, and nearly every one after that.

"He's still alive," was the answer Scott and Diana gave each time the subject was broached. Each time the doctors tried to point out that time was ticking away, that if Scott and Diana let the child live beyond twenty weeks, they'd have to treat him like a person. By state law, he warned, they'd have to go through the whole birthing process, file for a death certificate, and arrange for burial if he made it past twenty weeks.

"He has a soul," Diana said. "And I'm not God. I won't end his life."

So we waited, and cried together often, and prayed.

At twenty-three weeks, I went with Diana for her weekly ultrasound. They laid her on a paper-covered examining table, rubbed the gel on her skin, and rolled the transducer across her stomach.

We watched the screen. The baby's form appeared, as motionless as always. The technician moved the probe over Diana's stomach, back and forth, pressing into her skin.

He didn't say anything for a full minute, and then, quietly, with his eyes still on the screen, he said, "I'm not finding a heartbeat."

I held my breath while he tried again, pressing, rolling, searching. The room was silent.

After two more minutes, I watched as he set the transducer aside and turned off the screen. The man paused for just a second, then swiveled in his chair and faced Diana.

"I'm sorry…we knew this was coming. I'll get your doctor."

Diana's baby had died.

She had to carry him another week. For seven days, she lived with the knowledge that the baby inside her was dead. On Monday, she packed her things in an overnight bag and sat quietly while Scott drove her to Seattle. She checked into the hospital, changed into a gown, and laid on a bed without speaking while the doctor began the three-day inducement procedure.

Now it's Wednesday. Dave and I are here in this room to love Scott and Diana. We're here to cry with them, to pray, to listen to their questions and hope for answers. And Diana is holding out the baby she delivered less than an hour ago. He's only twenty-three weeks old.

"Do you want to hold my baby?" she asks.

I'm terrified. I don't know how I'll react. I don't want to hold him, because she might see that I'm afraid. She might see something on my face that hurts her.

125

In a fraction of a second, God whispers to my heart.

You are her one chance to show off her child. Take him in your arms.

"Of course I want to hold him," I hear myself say. God helps me reach out my arms. He gives me strength when I pull back the folds of blue blanket and look down at the tiny, not-yet-fully-developed face nearly hidden inside.

I smile at Diana through tears. "He's beautiful," I say.

And he is.

"His name is Simeon," she tells me.

"Hello, Simeon," I say. He weighs almost nothing. His lightness hurts my heart. He should be plump-cheeked and squalling—and I should be holding him at Diana's baby shower. I should be setting my pink lemonade punch on the table beside me, pushing torn gift wrap away with my feet, and cooing at him over the sounds of women chattering and laughing. I should have had to fight for my turn to hold him. Instead, I'm the only one. There are the men, looking at everything except each other, except at Diana and the baby. And there's me—the only woman Diana will ever hand her baby to.

I'm aware, in that second, that I may never have a higher honor in my life.

"I'm proud of you," I whisper to her.

She lets me hold him for several minutes, but I can tell she wants him back. I look once more into his sweet face and hand him carefully to his mother. She pulls the blanket away from his face and runs her finger lightly along his tiny brow.

"Did you see his feet?" she asks.

I tell her I didn't.

She uncovers them, holds them carefully between her fingers. They're small—unbelievably small—and they're perfect. I tell her so.

She looks at me, and then she looks at the baby in my arms. "I'm not afraid anymore."

"Not afraid?"

"I'm not afraid of heaven."

I ask her what changed.

"I've touched someone who is there, someone who will be waiting for me. Someday I'll see him again, and I'll hold him, and he'll be whole."

She adjusts the blanket so it covers his feet. She straightens the doll-sized blue knit cap over his head, and runs her hand along his tummy.

I watch her memorizing her child. She is a young woman with an old soul, and he is her gift—the gift God brought to release her from her fear and turn her eyes toward heaven.

The door opens and Diana's nurse comes in.

"I don't want to rush you…take all the time you want, but…"

"I'm ready," Diana says.

She looks once more into Simeon's little face and kisses his forehead.

"Goodbye, baby," she says, for the second time in her young life.

Eleven months later, I am in Diana's living room. I'm holding a fleecy blue bundle in my arms. The baby inside pushes hard against his blanket, kicking me in my stomach. I don't mind a bit.

His little fists beat the air; he twists and writhes and lets us all know how much he'd like to wriggle right out of his blanket. He puffs out his plump cheeks, grimaces, and sets up a wail.

His sister and brother lean against my arms, one on my left and one on my right.

"Luke's a noisy boy," Madison observes.

She's right. He's a noisy baby. And there's not a more beautiful sound in all the world.

15

Forget Me Not

"I will not leave you as orphans; I will come to you."

—John 14:18

*E*verything looks different up close. The buildings loom. The headstones, just small dots when viewed in quick glances from the freeway, have form and texture…and names. I sit in my car and wait for courage.

Ten years have passed since my mother's death—ten years to this very day. I wasn't here the afternoon they buried her. I wasn't here the day after, or the day after that. Weeks became months and months became years, and still I have stayed away. Until today.

"She's not there," I explained again and again, whenever concerned people asked why I hadn't visited her grave. "She's not there, so there's no point in going." After a while, courtesy or discomfort prevented anyone from broaching the subject with me. I welcomed their silence.

She left three daughters. At 26, I was the oldest. She left us suddenly…and she left on purpose.

Her death came at the onset of fall, the season she'd taught us to love best. When we were young she would open all the curtains at the first sign of rain and crack one window so we could sit together and smell the beauty of an autumn storm. We'd nestle together and count fluttering leaves and watch trees brush against the charcoal sky. She made us love storms. She taught us not to fear. I had trouble reconciling the irony: she, who had unfailingly prepared us to face life's tempests, left us unequipped to deal with her death.

"Your friends will come and go," she used to say, "but your family is forever." This was her standard bit of wisdom whenever someone hurt us. We'd cry on her shoulder and recount whatever betrayal we'd suffered. "I know," she'd say, hugging us and wiping our tears away. "Friends will let you down now and then, but you can count on family. We'll always be there for you." I believed her, right up until the day she took her life.

We staggered blindly for the first few days, clutching at each other, asking why. But then we began to take slow steps away from the nucleus of our grief, and like spokes on a wheel, we journeyed in opposing directions. One sister went the way of anger, and became as hard and unyielding as granite. The other sister chose tears, and became as soft and unstable as just-dug earth. I became, simply, numb. Because I feared the intensity of one emotion and the vulnerability of the other, I chose neither anger nor tears. I would not rant and rail against God. I would not dissolve in tears at the mention of her name. I chose instead to square my shoulders and lift my chin, to push the "unfortunate event" as far behind me as possible. With no experience to guide me, I attempted to guide my sisters toward my more rational choice. But they would not, or could not, follow. And so we isolated ourselves against one another, against the only other people on earth who could understand the depth of our shared loss.

Suicide. The word always brings to mind my high school English teacher, who delighted in expanding our vocabularies. A particular favorite of hers was the word "mellifluous." She'd say it slowly, as though savoring each syllable. "To flow off the tongue like honey. Smooth, euphonic, sweet-sounding. Mellifluous." Suicide is a mellifluous word—

deceptively, cruelly mellifluous. Where are the harsh consonants that should comprise such a devastating word? Where is the hard 'c' or 'k' that could convey the jarring jab of such an ugly reality? Instead, the word flows easily and softly, as though it should be describing a soothing fabric or a delicious new flavor of sorbet.

I could not speak that word for a full three years after my mother's death. Not since the afternoon, two days into our grief, when I found myself standing at a hospital information booth. I don't remember how I got to the hospital—I only recall waiting there, trying to formulate and rehearse my request before the volunteer on duty could turn and give me her attention. "Do you have a support group for survivors of suicide?" I intended to ask. The sterile, clinical environment seemed safe to me. Impersonal. I felt I might have the nerve to divulge my grief in such a setting.

But when the volunteer turned toward me, the words died on my lips. I knew the woman.

"Well, hey there! I haven't seen you in awhile. How've you been?" she asked with a wide grin.

I forced myself to return her smile. "Just fine," I lied.

"Can I help you with something today?"

She couldn't know. No one who had any inkling of who I was, or who my mother was, could ever hear that word associated with her name.

"Do you have the time?"

She looked at the oversized clock on the wall beside us, of which I had a clear, unhindered view, and announced that it was 3:15.

That was the last time—for a long time—I even considered speaking the word.

I lived for the most part in a state of denial. Mostly, I denied she ever existed. Sometimes I denied her death.

"How's your mom doing?" a teenage boy asked me, when I bumped into him at the mall two years later. Mom had been an advisor for his Junior Achievement group, and Robert had never hidden his affection for her. As so many of my own friends had done, Robert used to seek her out just for her listening ear.

He admired my mother; I didn't want him to stop. I couldn't let one act redefine her, like some horrid exclamation point at the end of her life.

"She's fine."

"Tell her I said 'Hi', okay?"

I promised to do so and walked away.

Occasionally, I ventured from my haven of denial and took timid cat-steps toward anger or sadness. I'd flirt with the very edge, peek over, then retreat quickly back to what I knew best.

We found out I was infertile a few months after her death. I needed her then, but I wouldn't allow myself the anger I felt I had a right to. Instead, I relied on my husband and our circle of friends. I didn't allow myself to cry a year later when I went shopping alone to pick out baby clothes for our soon-to-be adopted son—not even when I followed a mother and pregnant daughter from rack to rack, eavesdropping on a conversation that should have been mine.

The closest I came to anger was when Zachary turned four and asked me, one day, why he only had one grandma and his best friend had two. I knew what he did not—that he'd been deprived of an incredible, loving grandmother, one who would have tickled him mercilessly, baked whatever his heart desired, and pointed out stars on warm summer nights. One who loved to laugh, long and hard; one who loved to sing. She had robbed him. I wanted to hate her for that.

What little anger I allowed to seep out was never directed at her. Nor would I let myself feel anger toward God. Instead, I reserved my indignation for those who cast judgment.

"There's no forgiveness for those who commit suicide," a

131

woman announced during a Bible study one August afternoon.

The day was exceptionally warm. We'd brought in portable fans and opened all the windows. Our hostess served iced tea in a vain attempt to chase the heat. But nothing cooled me like her words.

My stare was frigid as she ran through her litany of reasons why those who took their earthly lives forfeited their eternal lives.

I didn't know her God. I didn't recognize my Savior as she described Him. I let her drone on about damnation, while my mind re-lived the night my mother came to Christ.

We'd gone for a walk, just Mom and I. Around the neighborhood, past the park, up the hill, and to a little corner grocery store where we bought ingredients for chocolate chip cookies. Back home, we baked together, and talked. Mostly I talked. I shared my Jesus with her, my newly found love. I'd tried to tell her many times before, but all previous attempts had been firmly resisted. On this night, though, she was soft—and her heart was wide open. The cookies were long cooled and the clock read 4:30 A.M. when I felt God prompting me to ask her if she was ready to meet Him. She was. I woke my sisters, who stumbled sleepy-eyed and overjoyed to the table. We formed a circle and prayed together. An hour later—at my mother's insistence—our youth pastor arrived and baptized her, just as the sun was rising over the lake.

We shared two precious years as Christians—mother and daughter, yet spiritual sisters. We'd laugh together in amazement at God's love for us. One night, while out enjoying a walk through the neighborhood, she said, "I couldn't do it."

"Do what?"

"Make the sacrifice God did. I couldn't love anyone enough to do that. I could never just hand over one of you girls for the sake of someone else."

She shook her head in wonder. "Can you believe what He did for us?"

I couldn't.

"Shannon?"

I looked up to see the women in my study group looking at me. The woman's tirade had ended. She sat with her Bible on her lap, staring at me and waiting for a comment. Or maybe she was waiting for applause.

"Don't you agree?" she asked.

I didn't, and I told her as much, with more furor than I'd intended. Never once did I mention my mother, though I could have. I could have easily described the joy I knew she was experiencing at that precise moment, while we fools below hashed out the mysteries of eternity and forgiveness.

Now I'm here. Her grave, I've been told, is directly in front of my car, seventh from the end. I can see it from where I'm sitting, though I can't make out the words.

I step out of the car before remembering to pick up the small bundle of flowers I collected from my garden. I sit down again slowly, stalling, and carefully rearrange the bouquet.

I'm afraid to make the short walk. My mind tells me it's just a marker. My heart tells me it's a door. For ten years I've barricaded the entrance, protecting myself from the memories within. I know the power of memories. Like water molecules, they draw themselves together, linking, growing, one upon the other. I feared I'd drown in the deluge.

My shoes are dark against the green, green grass. I skirt the graves respectfully and slow my steps as I edge closer. Five, six,...seven.

I don't look right away. Instead, I close my eyes and pray for strength to face whatever happens.

133

"Father? Please…don't let me be angry," I whisper.

He whispers back, I'm *here*.

"What if I can't stop crying?"

I'm *here*.

I open my eyes and let my fingers trace the letters as the first tears form. Her name is beautiful.

The locked door flies open, as I knew it would. But I am not assaulted by the thoughts I expected—the ugly, painful memories of her death and all the horror that followed. I understand, in an unexpected flash, what I have done. I have shielded myself from *all* my memories—all the good and all the bad—fearing that one would lead to another and back again. Fearing I'd never escape. I understand, because suddenly, I find myself standing under a downpour of memories I've missed.

I glance at the sky, and see the gray of her eyes. Leaves rustle against my feet, and I hear her laughter. The breeze against my cheek is cool, and I feel again the soft touch of her hand.

I remember.

I remember my friend. After all these long years of denying that I missed her, I sit and let myself remember.

And suddenly, there is no room for anger. How can I be angry at the woman who gave me wings, the woman who once told me, "I believe you can do it all?"

There's no room for sadness. How can I be sad when her darkness is over? When I know our separation is temporary?

There is only room for a sweet breath of gratitude. Leaning against the cool granite, I thank God for His gift to me. I thank Him for my joy and my delight, my sister, my friend, my teacher—my mother.

I place the forget-me-nots on her grave and spread their tiny blue blossoms against her headstone.

I won't forget.

Spring

"A time to plant…a time to be born"

I liked Hank the first moment I saw him, because he could not take his eyes off Joan. And that was appropriate. After all, he was the groom. And the view he had, standing there at the end of the church aisle, was of his bride—my beautiful, elegant friend, who crossed the distance between solitude and her new life with confident steps and a wide smile.

I'd been hoping for a Hank for several years, pretty much ever since I got to know Joan. In my opinion, she was too wonderful not to share with someone. She was smart and kind and gracious. She was lovely. She wrote books—good books—and loved to travel. She could carry on an interesting conversation on just about any topic. She was a great dessert maker and baker. The more I got to know her, the more I felt that someone should come along and sneak into Joan's heart.

It finally happened. Joan mentioned Hank one night, somewhat casually, during one of our writing critique group meetings. My head snapped up at the mention of a man. "Who's this Hank?" I wanted to know.

She tried to be nonchalant. "Just someone I knew a long time ago. I ran into him again recently. We've been emailing."

I didn't want to ruin the thing, so I tried to keep my

questions to a minimum. It was an exercise in patience, but it paid off. I began to hear Hank's name mentioned more and more frequently, and after a year of such hints, one day I walked out to my mailbox and found a wedding invitation waiting for me. Just like that.

People always cry at weddings. But when the two getting married are both widowers, and both in their sixties, and friends on both sides of the aisle feared their loved one might never take a chance again, the tears have extra meaning. There was a whole lot of sniffling going on in church that warm June afternoon. What I observed, I observed through a blur. But I still saw clearly. In a time that the world would call their "autumn years," Hank and Joan entered spring again.

Spring is the turn of a page. It's a new chapter, and a fresh start. It's stepping into the unknown with a sense of wonder and anticipation.

Spring can be as simple as the touch of someone's hand on your shoulder. Perhaps you've been living in a winter of regret. You've hurt or disappointed a loved one. Forgiveness taps you on your shoulder, and you turn to find compassionate eyes and the embrace of a friend. Spring is a clean slate.

Spring is a time of hidden work. Just as seeds are transformed below ground, so too, the work God performs on us is often unseen. In spiritual spring, we are being strengthened and prepared.

Sometimes, spring is an awakening. We creep along in the dead of winter, numbed by loss and pain, until a sudden breeze brings a fresh revelation from God. I lived in winter for months on end after my mother took her life, but I remember the second my soul stirred. I caught a scent of something on the wind, and closed my eyes and drew a deep breath. I remember feeling a surge of hope and a sudden love for life, when I'd been so long gone I thought I'd never care about anything else again. I realized I had much to live for. God had called me to life again, called me to step out of winter and rejoice in the spring He'd set before me.

When I began to organize this collection of stories, my natural impulse was to arrange them from spring to winter. That's how the seasons flow in my head. But when I took a second look, I knew I didn't want the book to end in winter. I wanted to remind you—and myself—that winter is never the end. Spring is the end, because when we stand before the Lord, we're going to enter an existence of perpetual newness, freshness, and revelation. Our spring with Him will be eternal.

The stories in this section all reveal God's whispers of encouragement through the newness of spring. A young girl begins a fresh chapter in a new adoptive home. An elderly woman understands grace for the first time in her life. Whether we're three or ninety-three, spring can break through winter's grayness and show itself in a sudden moment—and in ways that might surprise you. As you read these stories, I pray you'll let the God of second chances and new mercies draw you closer—and let Him lead you to spring.

16

My Girl

"For you have not received a spirit of slavery leading to fear again, but you have received the spirit of adoption as sons by which we cry out, 'Abba! Father!'"

—Romans 8:15 (NASB)

Spring arrived in October one year. It came in the shape of a three-year-old girl, who stood at the bottom of our porch steps glaring up at me with defiant green eyes.

"You're not my mommy, you know," was all she said. But it was enough to sink my heart.

I had been waiting for this day—this exact moment—for three months. Tera was coming to live with us. Though for the time being we were only her foster parents, our goal was adoption. I already thought of her as my daughter, but it was clear that Tera thought otherwise.

Earlier that year, while visiting my friend Kari one evening, she had asked if I'd like to see her newest foster daughter. I followed her up the stairs to a bedroom at the end of the hall. As she slowly pushed the door open, a shaft of light fell on tousled, straw-colored hair. Tera rolled over and flashed us a mischievous grin.

"Hey—you're supposed to be sleeping," Kari whispered.

Tera was lying on a tiny white toddler bed under an equally tiny quilt. Almost instinctively, I reached down and touched the top of her head, and as I did so I caught myself thinking, "Oh Lord, I would love for this to be my daughter."

The thought startled me. We were all done trying to adopt; there was no way I was getting back on that roller coaster. After a touch-and-go adoption with our son nine years earlier, we'd made thirteen different attempts to adopt again, and every time we had failed. The reasons varied, but generally the birth mothers had changed their minds—but not before we had begun bonding with their babies and dreaming of the life we'd have with each one. Each loss ripped open the wound of my infertility. We felt helpless and hopeless and frustrated, and in the end we'd concluded that perhaps God wanted us to be content with one child.

So I was surprised to find myself breathing that prayer. Still, I asked Kari about the plans for Tera.

"Will she be available for adoption, or is she going back to her mother?"

"Oh, she's going back. I don't expect I'll have her very long at all."

That was that, I thought. But I was wrong.

A few weeks after that conversation, Kari called me. "I know this is coming out of the blue, but would you consider adopting Tera?" she asked.

"In a heartbeat," I answered. Even as the words left my mouth, I realized I hadn't yet discussed the idea with Dave.

"Then you'd better get licensed, because they're starting a search for a foster-adopt home," Kari said.

"What about Tera's mom?"

"It looked at first as if she might stabilize, but things have been getting worse. She can barely take care of herself right now. The caseworker has decided it's in Tera's best interest to find her a permanent home."

After we hung up, I prayed. Later, Dave and I prayed together—and decided to try one more time.

We took fifty hours of classes in three weeks. I spent a

Saturday learning first aid and infant CPR, and then crammed for a written test about the dangers of AIDS. We endured four visits by a social worker in order to satisfy a home study. We got fingerprinted. We cleared out a room we'd been using for an office and turned it into a bedroom. Then we waited.

The call came unexpectedly one morning. "Well," the caseworker began, "two other families came forward and expressed interest in adopting Tera. After visiting the other homes and interviewing the other families, we've made our decision. We've chosen you."

I cried, and tried hard to believe it would happen this time.

At the social worker's suggestion, we began frequent visits at Tim and Kari's to get Tera used to us. Gradually, we began taking her to the park or out for ice cream. She went with us happily each time, but was just as happy to wave goodbye at the end of our visits. She'd been with her foster family for several months by this time, and she had no intentions of leaving.

So she wasn't pleased on that gray October afternoon when we came to pick her up. "Why are you giving them my clothes?" she asked Tim as he loaded two black garbage bags into our trunk.

"Tera, we talked about this, remember? You're going to be living with the Woodwards. But we'll see each other a lot, I promise."

My heart broke at the look on Tera's face. We were about to be her fourth home in three years. All the chaos in her young life had taught her to be a tough little girl. But there was no doubt that she was wrestling with her emotions now. She wanted to cry, but she wanted to look indifferent, too. The need to appear indifferent won out.

"I don't care," she said at last.

She sat rigid in the back seat during the ten-minute drive

home. We couldn't get her to talk, though we tried every topic we could think of.

It wasn't until she stood at the bottom of the stairs that she broke her silence.

"You're not my mommy, you know."

Oh, but I was. She just didn't know it yet.

She stood below me, a picture of contrast. At first glance, she looked like any other three-year old just coming back from a family outing. She wore jeans with ruffles along the pockets, and a little pink and white t-shirt with an appliqué of flowers across the chest and a dime-sized smudge of spilled lunch on her tummy. The tips of her blue sneakers were damp, as if she'd been out running across the grass.

You could almost think she was a typical toddler returning home on a typical afternoon, except for the fact that the heart beating under her shirt pulsed so furiously I could watch its rhythm. I could see the tempest brewing behind her green eyes, eyes the color of churning seawater. Her mouth had settled in a line of resolution, and the jut of her shoulders said, "I'll take care of myself."

Whether she wanted to accept it or not, this moment was the start of a new chapter in her life. This was her new beginning. She had a home—one she would never have to leave. She had a new family and a brand new identity. She was loved, even if she didn't want to be.

We looked at each other for a long minute, and then she shivered. She had refused to put her coat on when we left Tim and Kari's. Now the skies were loosening their grip on the rain, and a chilly gust of wind rippled through the chimes hanging above her head.

"Know what we could do? We could go inside and make some cocoa. Would you like to do that?"

"I hate cocoa," she said.

Not possible, I thought. "What about with marshmallows?"

She hesitated. "Are they little?"

I nodded. *Just like you.*

Another blast of wind drew a stream of gray smoke from our chimney and sent it spiraling across the roof. It whirled toward the stairs and wove itself between the two of us, burning our eyes with its acrid touch.

"I think Mommy Kari will come and get me in a while."

I didn't answer. I just walked back down the stairs and picked her up. Her body stiffened in my arms, deepening the hurt I felt. I wished I could make her believe she was safe with us. I wished I could convince her she was home.

She wouldn't sit by the fire Dave and Zac had built for her. She perched instead on the edge of a dining room chair and drank her cocoa steadily and quickly, glancing back at the door every few minutes as if waiting for someone to walk through and rescue her.

I finally coaxed her down the hall to look at her new bedroom. She gave it a cool once-over, her eyes stopping on the two black bags sitting near the bed. All she owned in the world sat here in this strange room.

"I like my other room better."

I had a flashback of the hour I'd spent at the home improvement store trying to pick out wallpaper for this room. After weighing my options, I had eventually narrowed my choices to two borders: one with pink and yellow roses, and one with scenes of Victorian bunnies sipping tea in a meadow. As if her very happiness hinged on the decision, I deliberated and debated, back and forth. The bunnies won, and now they graced the walls of Tera's room—a room she didn't want to live in.

Her gaze lingered on her bed, and I knew what she wasn't seeing. She wasn't noticing that the blue of her quilt exactly matched the wallpaper. She wasn't conscious of how many times I'd fluffed her pillows to make them look as inviting as possible. She wasn't seeing the two of us sitting together against the backboard, sharing a picture book. She wasn't anticipating the touch of my hand on her hair as I tucked her in.

"I hate this bed," she said. "I want my little bed at Mommy Kari's."

Oh, Tera, I thought, *please let me love you.*

"Shannon, can we call Mommy Kari?" she asked, first thing the next morning.

I wanted more from her. I wanted a smile, or a good morning hug. I wanted her to be glad to be sitting at my kitchen table, sharing pancakes with her new family. I didn't want to hear about Kari. And I didn't want to be Shannon. I wanted to be Mommy.

"We'll see."

"Or we could go visit her. Can we do that, Shannon?"

I stared at the three circles bubbling in the pan and decided to ignore her question.

"Did you have good dreams last night, Tera?" I asked instead.

"No."

I flipped the pancakes. "Ready for another one?"

She glared at me, a look I was starting to expect.

"I hate pancakes."

By the end of that month, I hated my name. I hated the way it sounded on her tongue.

Will I ever be Mommy? I wondered. I had asked God for nine years to bring us another child. I hadn't realized until now how much I loved being called Mommy. Every time Tera said my name, I felt the chasm between us. To her, I was just another adult in a series of caretakers. I wouldn't have even minded if she called me "Mommy Shannon," but she refused. As if she knew how much I wanted it and relished her power, she insisted on calling me, simply, Shannon.

I poured my heart out during my quiet time early one

morning. Everyone else was asleep; not even our rooster had roused yet. I curled up on our couch and cried.

"Lord, she doesn't see me as her mother."

"She longs for her old life."

"She's keeping a distance between us."

"She doesn't trust me."

Heaven was silent.

"What do I do, God?"

More silence.

"Lord?"

And then I heard His whisper. *Father.*

"What was that, Lord?"

Call Me Father.

"But You *are* my Lord."

Yes. But I'm also Abba. I'm also your Father.

I caught a glimpse of His heart in that second, and I knew how much He loved me. As He had done dozens of times before, He brought a perfect situation to reveal a part of His nature. He showed me the heart of a Father, who had gone to great lengths to adopt a child and wanted her to acknowledge who He was.

I closed my eyes and let His love wash over me. I drank it in, and let it calm me.

Then I asked again. "Father, what do I do about Tera?"

Keep loving her.

I kept on loving her. Over the next few months, I waited as patiently as I could. I hugged her and read stories to her and prayed that she'd adjust.

And then one morning, she smiled at me across the breakfast table.

"Did you have good dreams last night, Mommy?" she asked.

Only one. And it just came true.

17

Mirror, Mirror

"For if anyone is a hearer of the word and not a doer, he is like a man observing his natural face in a mirror; for once he has looked at himself and gone away, he has immediately forgotten what kind of man he was. But one who looks intently at the perfect law, the law of liberty, and abides by it, not having become a forgetful hearer but an effectual doer, this man will be blessed in what he does."

—James 1:23–25 (NASB)

The Christian bookstore was quiet and nearly empty. While I browsed through books, Zac tried to select one pencil from the dozens in the bin at his feet. Except for his rummaging noises and a running commentary— "This sparkly one looks like it would write the best, Mom" —the only other sound in the store was the muffled voice of the salesclerk on the phone.

Bright sunlight darted across the carpet as the front door of the store opened, drawing my attention to the two people walking in. The plaid-shirted, black-bearded man was tall and gruff-looking, so much so that I barely noticed the small woman at his side. The couple turned down the aisle parallel to ours, the aisle where the children's books were displayed.

I resumed my browsing, newcomers all but forgotten, until the door opened again and a small boy about three years old came rushing in. His mission was clear. His desperate look and telltale hopping indicated he was hunting for the bathroom. He had no trouble spotting his tall father above the racks of books. Rounding the corner of the aisle, he started to explain his need.

"Daddy, I have to…"

That's all he managed to say. His request was bitten in two by his father's explosive response.

"I thought I told you to stay in the van!"

My heart froze.

"But Daddy, I need…"

"Did you hear me?!" the man thundered. "Get yourself back to the van NOW!"

I nearly went to the van myself. Glancing down, I saw Zac watching the small boy through the racks. He turned solemn, disapproving eyes up at me and shook his head.

The door opened again as the boy left. This time the sunlight darting across the carpet seemed less bright to me. I looked at the salesclerk; she shrugged her shoulders as if to say, "What can you do?"

For several minutes there was absolute silence in the store. I couldn't get the boy out of my mind and couldn't understand how his father could scream at him one moment and browse through children's books the next. For a fleeting second I considered walking around the corner and pointing out the irony to him.

Before I could act on that impulse, the door opened again. I felt a moment of panic. I was afraid to look, afraid to see the boy's desperate expression again. But I risked a peek and saw that this time it was a girl a few years older.

"Dad…"

"Get!!" he bellowed.

This time every eye in the store turned and looked.

"But Dad…"

"Didn't you hear me? I told your brother, and now I'm telling you—stay in the van!"

She found a bit of courage from somewhere and tried one more time. "But Dad…he wants Mom. He needs to…"

"NOW!"

The girl slunk out, head down and cheeks flaming with embarrassment and frustration.

"Mom, can we go?" Zac whispered.

I nodded. Taking the pencil he hurriedly selected, I walked to the counter and fished out a dollar. The salesclerk shrugged at me again, shaking her head.

Zac followed and stood silently as the clerk gave me my change. I handed him the paper bag and we started toward the door.

As we neared the aisle filled with children's books, I turned my head and averted my eyes, which is why I didn't see what Zac was doing until my hand was on the door. I glanced down, expecting to see him at my side, and when I found that he wasn't, I looked back over my shoulder. I was shocked to see where he was. He had stopped in front of the children's book aisle, a mere five feet from the man and woman. He stood resolutely, his little feet wide apart and one arm straight out ahead of him, pointing a tiny finger directly at the man.

You could have heard a pin drop as Zachary spoke. In an unwavering voice, a voice completely devoid of fear, he made a firm and loud pronouncement:

"THAT is a foolish man!"

My son, the prophet. I wanted to scream, "Run, Zac, run!" but the words wouldn't budge past the rock in my throat.

He stared at the bewildered man for a long second before turning and calmly following me out the door. With great difficulty, I resisted the urge to check over my shoulder as we made our way to the car.

We buckled up in silence. I was stuck in an awkward spot, and I knew it. On the one hand, I wanted to take Zac out for ice cream and buy him a medal. I wanted to applaud his

147

bold defense of the little boy. After all, he had spoken the truth. He had echoed the thoughts of everyone in that store. But we had never allowed or encouraged him to correct adults. My mind raced, wondering what I could—or should—say.

I didn't have long to squirm. Zac took the conversation in hand.

"Mom, do you think we should pray for that man?"

To say that I was pleased would be an understatement. We would still have to have a little talk about the inappropriateness of children correcting adults, but Zac's concern gave me a great measure of relief. Somehow, his young heart knew that prayer should follow such exhortation.

"Yes, honey," I said, reaching for his hand. "How about if you pray for him?"

He closed his eyes into tight, squinty lines. "Dear Jesus, please help that foolish man to be nicer to his kids. You know, Jesus, that boy just needed to go to the bathroom. Amen."

Zac opened his eyes and gave me a perplexed look. "Mom, that man didn't even let his boy talk. He just said no. Why did he do that, Mom?"

I didn't have an answer, but I spent a good part of that day thinking about his question and wondering what life must be like in that home.

That night, just before dinner, Zac slammed the back door and ran into the kitchen panting.

"Mom, can I have…"

I spun around and faced him with hands on my hips.

"No, Zac, now listen: I told you already, you've had enough snacks this afternoon. Nothing more for you until we eat dinner. Now please—stop asking."

His expression was hurt and a little indignant.

"I wasn't gonna ask for a snack. I just want some string to make a belt."

"Oh." I dug through the junk drawer and found a ball of twine. "Will this do?" I asked quietly.

He thanked me and ran back outside, quickly forgetting my offense.

But I didn't.

As I walked toward the window to watch, I caught my reflection mirrored in the glass.

"That," I whispered, "is a foolish woman."

Without waiting to hear Zac's full request, I had assumed he was about to beg for yet another snack. Granted, he had already asked me three times since lunch. And no, I hadn't yelled at him. I had even been polite. But that was all beside the point. The word "no" had jumped out of my mouth so swiftly, I hadn't even given him the chance to finish his question.

How many times have I done that? I wondered. *How often do I answer before I've really given him a chance to speak? Do I just say no out of habit, or is it because I don't think his requests are valid?*

Something about the whole topic twitched my memory. I knew I had just read something along those lines. I thought for a moment, and then a flicker of recognition ran through my mind. During my quiet time, only a day or two before, I'd come across a verse in Proverbs about this. I grabbed my Bible, opened it quickly and reread the words.

"He who answers before listening—that is his folly and his shame" (Proverbs 18:13).

Conviction struck me. Today it was a minor, forgivable mistake; but what happens to a lifetime of such errors? *What do I miss, every day, in my haste to say no to my son?* I wondered.

"Lord," I prayed. "Help this foolish woman. Teach me how to really listen before I answer, and give me the grace to say yes to the little things that mean so much to Zac."

I turned the oven temperature down, slipped on my shoes, and headed outside. The sound of hammering and muffled voices drew me toward the shed. As I approached unnoticed, I saw my son and husband bent over the work-bench.

"Right here's where you want to put in that second nail." Dave said to Zac. He handed him a hammer. "Give it a good smack."

Zac raised the hammer with both hands and delivered four or five good taps, connecting two thin pieces of wood together. He grinned at his dad, then noticed me standing in the doorway. His eyes lit up—and I marveled for the thousandth time at how loving and forgiving children could be.

"Look at this, Mom! Dad helped me make a sword!"

"So you did."

He slipped the new weapon into the twine belt around his waist and smiled with satisfaction. "Dad said we could play for a while before dinner. He's Robin Hood and I'm his son."

Reassured that all was well between us, I decided to head back to the house to finish dinner preparations. I couldn't resist brushing his hair back before turning to leave.

"All right," I said over my shoulder, "but you boys shouldn't play too long. Dinner's almost ready."

A warm hand on my arm stopped me.

"Don't go yet!" Zac pleaded. "I have a great idea! Why don't you be Maid Marian, and you can get stuck somewhere and we'll rescue you. Please, Mom?"

My thoughts drifted for the briefest second to all that awaited me in the kitchen. In my mind's eye I saw plates waiting to be set out for dinner and a salad waiting to be prepared. I saw...my reflection mirrored in the window.

And then, I heard the Lord. *Start today. Start right now.*

I looked down at my son's eager face. It mattered to him. I wondered how many of my prayers were of such stuff—silly little things that wouldn't amount to much in the scheme of life, but things I brought before my Father anyway. Things He granted, just because He loves me.

"Okay, Zac," I agreed. "But only if you help me make a pointy hat."

18

Ellie

"These things I have written to you who believe in the name of the Son of God, so that you may know that you have eternal life."
—1 John 5:13 (NASB)

My maternal grandmother, Mickey, frequently spent Saturday afternoons visiting and bringing small gifts to the residents of local nursing homes, and because she believed that charity should be modeled to children, she often took me with her. I was convinced she was an angel. I had no desire to be an angel, but I loved my grandmother—and loved being with her—so I went without protest.

"Which one today?" I'd ask as we backed down the driveway.

"Bethany," she'd sometimes answer. I'd run through the files in my mind in anticipation of the people we'd see there. Bethany Home had a woman with long silver hair who always sat in the same chair near the front door, holding a box of tissues and cleaning a section of the adjacent wall. There were no smudges on that wall, but she scrubbed them anyway.

On other Saturdays our destination was the Josephine Home, or "Josie," as my grandmother called it. Crazy Bill lived there. He was a diabetic man in a rusty wheelchair who thought I was his little sister. He'd see me coming from the top of the ramp, where he perched most afternoons to watch the goings-on up and down the connecting hallways.

"Bettina!" he'd call, latching eyes with mine. "Come and play with me, Bettina!"

I'd clutch Grandma's hand tightly as our footsteps crossed the distance between us and the wheelchair.

Grandma would pat his shoulder and greet him cheerfully. "Gorgeous day, isn't it, Bill?"

Crazy Bill, I'd correct her silently. He scared the life out of me. His legs were gone, but his arms were strong. He pulled himself along the rail that threaded the walls from one end of the nursing home to the other, back and forth, never seeming to tire. Whenever he paused in his travels, he'd pluck at the front of his bathrobe with nails that were long, chipped, and yellowed—trying, like the silver-haired woman at Bethany, to remove something that wasn't there. I would stare at his hands with a mixture of fascination and dread, fearing that one day those hands might clutch my arm and pull me into his embrace.

No matter how kind Grandma was, Bill found a way to yell at her. I didn't understand how she kept it up.

"Your blanket slipped a bit. Can I straighten it for you, Bill?"

He'd scowl and begin barking in that raspy voice. "I'll do it myself! Let me do it myself!"

Grandma just kept smiling, but I shrank from his voice.

She tried to help me understand. "People don't like to lose control, honey. That's all it is."

Every once in awhile, she'd tell me Bill's story in an effort to alleviate my fear. "He was in the war, you know. I've seen pictures of Bill in his uniform. He was quite handsome. It's a shame his mind gave out on him."

It didn't help. No stories about the war could cover the aroma of urine and pain and fear that permeated the corridors of that nursing home and all the others we visited.

We'd step through those doorways into a world of haunted eyes and shrieks and grimaces. And the whole thing terrified me.

At a fairly young age, my grandmother fell victim to severe rheumatoid arthritis and stopped venturing out. Her angel visits came to an end, and the tables turned. She was now the shut-in, and people began coming by with gifts and goodies for her. Most of my Saturdays were spent at her side, watching reruns of *Bonanza* and playing Old Maid when her hands allowed her to hold the cards. I never went inside another nursing home, not while she was living, and not after she passed away.

So I wasn't sure how to react, twenty-some years later, when my husband came home from meeting with his seminary advisor and told me he'd been asked to pastor in a nearby retirement center. The term sounded suspiciously like a nursing home. The old smells rushed from the back of my brain and flooded me with dread.

"Do you need me to be there with you?" I asked, hoping he'd suggest that I stay home and bake…or scrub the toilet…or change the oil in the truck.

"Of course," he said, smiling. "It's just going to be me and a dozen elderly ladies. I think they'd like to have you there."

That wasn't the answer I hoped to hear. I wanted him to shoulder this one alone. I wanted him to say, "I'll be fine without you. You stay home." But he didn't know what I was thinking. I felt suddenly very ashamed of my repulsion.

So I went. That first Sunday, I put on Grandma's cheerful smile and my best blue dress, and tried hard to shove my fears aside. But I held Dave's hand as we approached the building, just the same.

I tensed as the automatic doors opened before us and we stepped into the lobby. I expected to smell death and pain and fear, the same cloudy essence I'd stored in my memories. But the smell that greeted me was floral, and pleasant.

A generous arrangement of yellow roses stood tall in a crystal vase just inside the lobby. That was my first surprise. I didn't remember ever seeing roses in the nursing homes of my childhood.

This place was clearly not a nursing home. There was an air of grace and grandeur I had not expected, but as I looked around at the plush mauve sofas and their matching pillows, the untouched magazines splayed out fan-like on the smudgeless glass coffee table, and the framed artwork adorning the walls, I had a notion that this grandeur was a bit canned. I suspected that if I walked into another of this chain's retirement homes, I'd find the same painting of the canal in Venice hanging on the same wall of the same mauve-toned lobby.

I heard no shrieks. Instead, live piano music wafted over the balcony. I saw no grimaces on the faces of the few residents walking through the lobby. But I could feel the anticipation of death, just the same.

We walked through double doors at the back of the lobby and into a meeting room. A dozen ladies sat waiting for us in teal-backed chairs. Dave walked around to face them.

"Hello," he said, smiling. Soft voices returned his greeting. He introduced me, and I smiled and nodded as I took a seat on the end of the second row.

He explained how we came to be there, told them he was glad for the chance to meet and get to know them, and asked them to open their Bibles to the Book of Romans. Then he prayed.

"Father, this book tells us of Your doctrine of grace. Please open our hearts and our minds to understand the truth You've written here. Amen."

As Dave began reading and explaining from chapter one, I snuck glances at the ladies. Two in particular intrigued me.

The first was Ann. Though I didn't know it at that moment, Ann would become very precious to me. She would take me under her wing, pray for me, and love me in a way no one had since my grandmother.

She sat tall in her chair, though she wasn't a tall woman. Her cream linen suit and matching pearls gave her an air of refinement, but as I studied her I became convinced that hers was not an elegance one put on in the morning and took off again in the evening. Hers was an elegance of character.

I noted that the Bible she held had pencil marks along the margins. The edges were curled and grayed from use; the maroon satin marker that dangled off the edge was frayed. She sensed my perusal and glanced at me, with eyes that looked right into my heart. I liked her immediately.

Sitting next to Ann was Ellie. She, too, sat straight and tall in her chair, but my impression of her was wholly different. Ellie seemed rigid, guarded, walled-up. When I caught her eye, I saw fear.

She didn't open her Bible. Instead, she trapped it against her orange and yellow flowered dress, careful to keep its cover closed. She didn't move at all, except to put a tissue to her mouth now and then, when a cough overtook her.

She listened intently to Dave, but more than once I caught a flicker of puzzlement crossing her expression. I wondered at Ellie's story.

Near the end of our time, Dave asked if anyone had any prayer requests. One woman asked for prayer for her unsaved daughter, another mentioned a grandson. A third said she'd been having pains in her eyes.

Ann leaned toward Ellie and I heard her say, "Let's ask for prayer for that cough of yours, Ellie."

Ellie shook her head. "I'm fine. It's nothing."

It wasn't nothing. Ellie coughed all through the study the following week, and the week after. Ann had invited us to stay and share dinner with her in the dining room that evening. She tried to get Ellie to join us, but she refused.

"She won't go to the doctor, you know," Ann said when we were seated.

"Why not?" I asked.

"She's frightened about what she might hear."

"But it's just a cough. Surely she doesn't think she'll die from a simple cough," I said.

Ann smiled. "The biggest fear among the people here is not that they might die, but that they might get moved to a nursing home."

I didn't blame them.

"No one wants to admit when they're feeling under the weather. They'll hide their ailments or downplay their physical pain as long as they can," she explained further. "They know that once they leave here, they've given up control of themselves."

Ann spoke the words, but I heard my grandmother's voice. *People don't like to lose control, honey. That's all it is.*

I worried about Ellie all week. By the following Sunday, I was determined to make her see a doctor.

"Ellie," I began, just after the study, "you're not getting better. You really need to see someone about your cough."

She actually coughed as she argued with me. "I know my own body and I'll decide when I need a doctor."

A few nights later, Ann called Dave.

"They took Ellie to a nursing home this afternoon."

"Oh, no," Dave began. "Her cough got bad enough for that?"

"No. She fell in her bathroom and broke her hip. She couldn't move to call for help, and it was several hours before one of the staff got suspicious and went to check on her."

"How long will she be in the nursing home?"

Ann's hesitation said more than her words. "That will depend on how she recovers. She needs to be in a place

157

with 24-hour care, at least for the time being. Pastor, she's quite upset about all this. Do you suppose you could go and see her?"

We dropped Zac off at a friend's house and followed Ann's directions to the nursing home. As we pulled into the parking lot, I thought I saw a silver-haired person sitting in a chair by the front door.

"Dave…would you mind if…can I stay in the car?"

He didn't answer at first. He just studied my face for a moment. "Why don't you pray for her while you're out here? Pray for me, too."

I sat in the darkness and stared out the window. I didn't pray at first. I just sat there and felt ashamed of myself.

Finally, I told Him. "I don't want to go in there."

I knew He knew. But I needed to say the words.

"I just don't want to go in there. It frightens me."

What are you afraid of?

It took a long time to find my answer. When I did, I surprised myself.

"I'm afraid someday I'll be the one in a place like this."

In a rush of warmth, I felt the Lord's presence. It was almost as tangible as if His arms were there enfolding me.

And if that happens, I'll be there with you.

I started to cry. I knew I needed to go inside, but I didn't know what I could say to Ellie that would make her feel better about being in that place.

I'll tell you what to say.

The lobby was empty; I could see that much from the walkway. But the smell I remembered rushed me as I pulled open the door, just as I knew it would.

A large woman in a pink nurse's shirt covered with cat pins directed me to Ellie's room. From outside the closed door, I could hear crying.

I went inside. She barely noticed my arrival.

"I'll die in here. I know it."

Dave shook his head. "You don't know that, Ellie."

"No one ever comes back from these places. It's where we all go to die." She turned her head slightly, dropping tears on her pillow.

"Let's pray together," Dave suggested.

"I don't pray anymore." At that, Ellie began crying harder. "I haven't prayed in three years—not since my husband died."

We let her talk, and I began to understand what had Ellie so walled up. When her husband became sick she prayed non-stop, and she prayed fervently. But when he died anyway, she became so angry at God that she stopped talking to Him. She stopped reading her Bible. She stopped doing everything her 90 years of church going had taught her to do. Now, her anger at God had changed to fear. She was afraid she had gone too far, and she was terrified to meet Him face to face.

I understood why I was there. Oh, Dave could have told her. But this was my issue, too. And I did have the answer.

The Book of Romans was my book. I'd been reading it through every week for three years, and somewhere in that time, my view of God had changed. Somewhere in those pages, I had let go of my own fear that I was a big disappointment to God.

"Ellie, do you believe that because you've ignored God for so long, He wants nothing to do with you now that you need Him?"

"That's exactly what I think."

We hadn't reached chapter five yet in our Sunday study, and I truthfully didn't know if Ellie would ever make it back to the group. But this was the night for her to see God's passion for her.

I opened the little Bible I kept in my purse. "Listen to this, Ellie: 'For when we were still without strength, in due time Christ died for the ungodly. For scarcely for a righteous man will one die; yet perhaps for a good man someone would even dare to die. But God demonstrates His own love toward us, in that while we were still sinners, Christ died for us'" (NKJV).

"Do you know what that means?" I asked.

She shook her head.

"It means that He saw you helpless and hopeless and He chose you in that condition. It means that when you were head over heels in love with your sin, God looked down and said, 'I want that one for Myself.'"

Dave nodded. "It means He knew exactly what He was getting and He saw those three silent years long before you even thought to get mad at Him. And still He wanted you."

"I know you feel out of control," I said. "You feel you have no strength and you can't help yourself. But according to what we just read, God died for the helpless. He loves you and He wants to cover you with His own righteousness. He wants to take away your fear and fill you with peace."

Ellie began crying again, but this time her tears were different. In the next hour, as Dave shared more about the incredible grace of God, Ellie's face relaxed and her eyes took on a look of hope.

We came back for several visits in the next few weeks. Though the leaves outside Ellie's window let go of the trees and piled themselves in orange and gold heaps, inside her room, new life blossomed. In the last days of her life, Ellie had a renewal of her spirit. She grabbed hold of grace, held it up at eye-level, and gazed at it in astonishment and wonder.

"In all my years, no one ever told me before that God was pleased with me just because of Jesus," she said the last time I saw her.

Ellie died just a few days after her 93rd birthday, on a day when the winds howled and rain spattered against her nursing home window.

But where she went, it was spring.

19

A Little Grace, Please

"If you, O LORD, kept a record of sins,
  O LORD, who could stand?
But with you there is forgiveness."

—Psalm 130:3–4

I shouldn't have let it bother me. When I heard the reason a new family gave for deciding to leave our church, I probably should have just laughed it off. But I couldn't.

"They're leaving because their son is afraid of Tera?! You mean...*our* Tera?"

"The one and only." Dave shrugged off of his coat and dropped it on the couch. "I asked if they'd be willing to stay and work it out, but they said no. They've made up their minds."

"But...but...Brandon is bigger and taller...and at least six months older than Tera! What could she possibly do to frighten him?"

"All they'd say was that he didn't want to come to Sunday school for fear of seeing Tera in class. They didn't elaborate and they didn't want to talk about it anymore."

I couldn't believe what I was hearing. I knew that among the five-year-olds, Tera had a reputation for being a tad bossy, but she wasn't mean-spirited. If she was guilty of anything at all it was usually trying to mother the other kids too much. What did this mean? Was this just a horrible new stage?

I spent most of that week worrying—and fuming a bit, if the truth be told. I wished the family had given us a little warning. Maybe we could have fixed the problem together.

And I wished they'd shown Tera a little grace. We talk about grace all the time as a fellowship. Dave weaves the theme throughout his messages. The men exhort one another to show grace at home. During my own teaching with the women's ministry I encourage the women to be vessels of grace to their husbands and children. How had that message been missed?

On Thursday of that week, Zac reminded me that everyone was meeting at Paula's for afternoon Bible study. It wasn't the study that interested him; it was the large group of kids he knew would be there. Paula's house was usually crawling with kids on Thursday afternoons.

"Can we go today, Mom?" he pleaded.

We didn't normally go. We were homeschoolers back then, and not always as disciplined as I would have liked. I'd make ambitious plans to get all our schoolwork done by lunch, and inevitably something would cause us to career off course. We'd get too involved in a biology lesson, or find the book we were reading together so fascinating, we'd read four chapters instead of one. Something always seemed to prevent us from making it to the study.

"Do you think we can get all our work done on time?" I asked.

He nodded optimistically and set to work.

Just before 2:00, Zac finished the last assignment, so the three of us piled into the truck.

"Hey! Nice surprise!" Paula greeted us at the door. "Kids are around back," she instructed my two.

We were nearing the end of our study about an hour later when we heard a shriek. One of the boys ran in. "Josh is

162

hurt!" Paula ran outside to check on her youngest. In less than a minute, she was back, carrying him in her arms. The entire side of his head was covered in blood.

"What on earth happened?!" One of the women ran to get a wet towel.

Josh's oldest brother, Theo, made the announcement. "Tera hit him on the head with a broom."

His words knocked the wind out of me. "She *what*?"

"She picked up a broken broom and *whack*! She smacked him right on the head."

I went to the back yard. My displeasure solidified into outright anger at the sight that met my eyes: Tera, blithely swinging on the jungle gym—and *singing*. She didn't look the part of a mad broom wielder…but there were witnesses.

"Young lady, you get over here this instant."

A startled look swept over her face at the sound in my voice. She slowed her swinging, then stopped altogether. With small and deliberate steps, she made her way to where I stood.

"What happened here?" I demanded.

She drew a big breath, signifying that the explanation was going to take every bit of energy she possessed. "Well, it was like this, Mom." She brushed a tendril of blonde hair away from her eyes, then gestured dramatically as if she were an eyewitness giving her account to a television reporter. "I was standing over there. Alex decided to get into the play car. And then that…that…Josh," she said in an exasperated tone, "tried to *push* Alex off the deck. He was going to hurt her, Mom—on purpose."

The look she gave me was one of pure vindication—as if she'd had every right to smack Josh on the head.

I glanced down at my feet and saw the offending broom. Picking it up, I scrutinized the jagged edges of the broken end.

"So you decided to hurt him first?"

163

She nodded.

I could feel my anger rising. "Well, that was a very, very bad decision."

She gulped. I don't think she'd considered that possibility.

"You get your coat, you apologize to Josh, and then you march yourself out to the truck."

She got her coat. She apologized to Josh. She marched to the truck.

I felt ill. Paula, on her way out the door to take Josh to the walk-in clinic for stitches, was kind and much more understanding than I think I would have been. "I'm sure Tera didn't realize what would happen," she said. "She thought she was protecting Alex."

I wasn't comforted. Nor did I feel better when another woman tried to console me. "This isn't the first trip to the walk-in clinic during Bible study," she laughed. "It's getting so those receptionists start looking for us on Thursdays afternoons."

As I got in the truck, Tera whispered, "I'm sorry, Mom."

I didn't believe her.

"Sorry? You sure don't look sorry. But you *should* be sorry, Missy."

We had made previous plans to meet up with Dave and another family at a nearby restaurant for dinner. All the way there I lectured Tera.

"What's happening to you? When did you start getting mean with the other kids? What were you thinking? Do you know how embarrassed and upset I am? What do you think Paula is feeling right now, as her little boy is getting stitches in his head? A broom? A broom, Tera? What was going through your mind when you picked up that broom and started swinging?"

She didn't answer a single question. I didn't let her. I didn't stop long enough to draw breath until we pulled into the restaurant parking lot and I turned off the truck's engine. Then I looked at her. But she wasn't looking at me now. She stared straight ahead through the windshield, as though she was observing the most fascinating vision out there in the parking lot.

Her stoicism, viewed through the lens of my anger, looked like pure stubbornness.

We sat in silence for several moments. Even Zac was quiet, though something on his face told me he was mulling over the possibility of defending his sister. Something on my face told him he'd better not.

In the silence, I thought with horror about the family leaving our church. Was this the sort of incident that had pushed them out our door? Had Tera done something vicious to Brandon too? My mind raced. Is this how people were going to start referring to us now? "Oh, you know—that church down the street; the one with the scary pastor's daughter. She little, but she's dangerous."

I glanced down at Tera again. She hadn't moved a muscle.

I began a silent prayer. "Oh, Lord, help me think of something I can say that will have an impact—something that will reach through to her."

It took a minute to hear His answer. In that time, I'd already begun formulating a new lecture. I decided to describe for her the steps involved in giving someone stitches. But the Lord stopped me cold.

I always know when He's talking to me in the midst of a crisis, because what He says runs so sharply counter to what I'm thinking. This occasion was no different.

He whispered, *Grace.*

And then, because I was so confused, He whispered it again. *Grace.*

I wanted to fight His voice, but I couldn't. While I struggled, He continued to reveal Himself to me.

She wants to be forgiven.

She's ready to come to Me.

You're standing in the way.

That last one did it. I had a vision of my daughter, reaching for the outstretched arms of Jesus—and me standing between them, blocking her every move.

My heart hurt.

It took a moment to find the right words.

"Tera? Zac? I owe you both an apology."

Their heads swiveled toward me.

I locked eyes with Tera. "Are you sorry for what you did?"

She nodded.

"Then the only person you need to go to is Jesus. He's ready—right now—to forgive you."

We held hands. I let her pray.

"Oh, Jesus," she said, "please help me to be a better girl." She sobbed. My little stoic, stubborn girl let loose the tears she'd been barely holding in.

I undid her seatbelt and drew her up on my lap. We cried together, and after a few moments, I felt all the tension drain out of her little body.

We heard a van door shutting.

"There's Chris and Cora," Zac said.

Our friends had arrived. Their little boy—another Josh—stood outside the van, waving at Tera.

"Are you ready to go out and see your friend?" I asked. She gave me a bright smile and hopped out of the truck.

Guilt kept me sitting where I was.

"Aren't you coming?" Chris asked.

I nodded. "I'll be there in a minute. Do you two mind if Zac and Tera go in with you?"

I watched my children walking toward the restaurant with our friends, and as I did so, I kept replaying my harsh words. How could I have been so severe, so unyielding?

It occurred to me—in a flash—that I could describe grace

166

to my children every day for the next twenty years, and it wouldn't mean a thing until I began to demonstrate it to them with my life.

My heart felt very heavy. But then, while I watched, Tera started skipping. She said something to Josh, threw her head back, and lifted her hands high in the air. Giggling, they skip-raced each other up to the door of the restaurant.

Don't you want to be forgiven, too? the Lord asked.

Did I want the same lightness of being, the same freedom I just observed in my daughter? Did I want her joy, her fresh start? Did I want to be unburdened?

"Yes, Father."

I turned, in my mind, and saw that nothing barred the way. His arms were open to me, too, and there wasn't a single thing between the two of us.

I stepped out of the truck and started across the parking lot. Inside, I was skipping.

20

Ready, Set... Wait

"'For I know the plans I have for you', declares the LORD, 'plans to prosper you and not to harm you, plans to give you hope and a future.'"
—Jeremiah 29:11

It all began harmlessly enough.

"Mom, Andy got a new shirt," my son announced one afternoon. "It's an army shirt with cool green and brown spots all over it."

I'd seen the cool army shirt and I told him so.

"Don't you think I'd look really, really good in a shirt like that?" he pressed.

The shirt actually seemed a bit loud to me, what with all those earthy splotches. But he didn't need to know that.

"Yes, Zac. I'm sure you'd look great in an army shirt."

That was the beginning.

We were out shopping one afternoon, and there it was—an army shirt, right on the rack in front of us, hanging there waiting for Zac to come and get it. It was loud, splotchy, and very cool. But once home, we discovered it didn't go well with sweat pants or jeans, so back we went the next day for matching pants. That led to army boots, because his blue and white sneakers didn't look right sticking out from beneath all that brown and green.

"There. You're all set," I said when we returned from our boot-hunting mission.

Zac shook his head. "Andy has camouflage underwear, too."

"But who sees a soldier's underwear?" I protested.

He gave me one of his "trust-me-I-know-best" looks. "A soldier has to *feel* ready for the war, Mom."

Now we were preparing for war—all because Andy had to go and show Zac his cool army shirt.

We found the underwear. Before getting out of the store we also found a camouflage undershirt and a bandanna.

Before I knew what was happening, friends and family caught wind of Zac's newest obsession and decided to help. Friends and family shouldn't do that.

One brought a camouflage wallet and matching key chain. Another showed up with a dog tag—a dog tag engraved with my baby's name on it. Still another sent him a subscription to a hunter-type catalog with scary, angry-looking green and brown men on the cover and pictures of over-priced gadgets inside.

Another brought him a black and white glossy of John Wayne—holding a rifle in one hand and a cigarette in the other.

"I...don't know quite how to thank you, James," I said through gritted teeth.

"No problem," he answered, oblivious to my distress.

James also loaned Zac a John Wayne war movie. We watched it every day for a week, just long enough for the Duke to start sneaking into my dreams.

Zac's seventh birthday was later that month. When we asked what he wanted to do for the day, it was no surprise at all when he suggested a trip to a nearby army/navy surplus store. As he was already the best-accessorized soldier in three states, we limited him to one item from the store. And it couldn't be a big sharp knife or a grenade.

He chose a helmet. It weighed half as much as Zac did and engulfed his head when he tried it on, but he was ecstatic.

He staggered under its weight all the way to the car, grinning from helmet-covered ear to helmet-covered ear.

I thought that was the end until a delivery truck arrived at our door with gifts from Zac's adoring aunties: an authentic army jacket and a set of brown, green, and black face paints.

Later that night, I crept into his bedroom and wiped a lingering smudge of green paint off one ear. I watched him sleeping, surveyed his bounty, and figured that by morning he'd probably be cured of military madness and onto something new. That's the way it usually worked. Generally, once we accumulated every last item for his latest collection, he lost interest and would begin the hunt for a new obsession.

So I was surprised when, the next morning, the soldier greeted me at breakfast in full gear.

"Where are you heading dressed like that?"

"Johnny's going to play *Taps* on his trumpet this morning. I told him I'd be there to help."

I watched out the window as he made his way across the field to meet our young neighbor at the jungle gym. While Johnny tripped over the notes to *Taps*, Zac stood straight and tall, saluting the miniature flag Johnny had stuck on top of the monkey bars.

Pretty soon Johnny had a cool, splotchy army shirt, too.

Soon after that, the neighbor kids started calling Zac "G.I. Joe"—and he didn't mind.

It wasn't ending. In fact, it was getting worse. Food was no longer food, it was "rations." His bedroom became "the barracks." He wouldn't come in the house if I simply called out the window—I had to use special walkie-talkies to communicate. Clearing the table was "KP duty." He didn't say it to my face, but I think behind my back he was referring to me as the "drill sergeant."

Then, one morning, he made an announcement.

"Mom, I want to join the army."

As if his father and I and all the neighbors didn't already

170

know that. "Yes, Zac, I know you do. And you never can tell. You may still be interested when you're eighteen. Until then…"

"No, Mom. I mean I want to join right now. Today."

"But, honey," I began, not wanting to be the bearer of bad news but secretly relieved that the army has age requirements, "they won't let you join when you're seven years old. You have to wait until you're eighteen."

He shook his head and pressed his mouth into a determined line. "That's everybody else. They'll let me in—they just have to see how bad I want to be a soldier."

"Oh, honey…"

"Mom, please!"

His face silenced me. It was plain to see how much he loved the whole thing. I didn't want to be the one to let him down, to crush all his hopes, to squash his dreams.

I decided to let the army do it for me.

"Okay, Zac. You get yourself ready and I'll drive you to the recruiting center."

Before you could say, "Left, right, left," we were in the car, heading downtown.

Two images are forever imprinted on my brain from that moment when we first stepped out of the car. One was the look on Zac's face as he straightened his jacket, adjusted his helmet and threw back his little camouflaged shoulders. He was the picture of absolute confidence.

The other image was the scene I observed through the large glass window of the recruiting center. Several men were at work inside. One, putting a file inside a cabinet, caught a glimpse of us through the window. The file stopped in mid-air. He must have said something to the others, because all heads turned in our direction. We were greeted with a roomful of half-hidden grins.

"Can we…help you?" the man behind the desk asked.

I looked at Zac, waiting for him to give the man his spiel.

Zac stood frozen.

"Isn't there something you want to say, honey?" I immediately regretted the "honey." If I was going to be the mother of a real, honest-to-goodness, gun-toting soldier, I'd have to remember not to embarrass him in front of his soldier friends.

"You." He whispered the word out of one corner of his mouth.

I cleared my throat. "My son...uh...wants to join the army. Right now."

Muffled laughter erupted from behind a manila folder. The man holding it to his face walked quickly around a corner and disappeared.

I continued. "I tried to explain about the age requirement, but Zachary is pretty sure you'll let him in when you see how badly he wants it."

To his credit, the man behind the desk didn't laugh or even smile. Oh, he wanted to. I could see it dancing in the corners of his eyes. But he was a well-trained soldier and withstood the temptation.

"That's great, son. We're always looking for good men."

Zac stood a bit taller.

"Your mom's right, though, about the age requirement. You do need to be eighteen, I'm afraid."

I snuck a glance, afraid of what that news might do to Zac. But he just gave a quick nod.

The man continued. "There are a couple of things I want you to do between now and then."

His first orders. I felt so proud.

"First, do your best in school. Learn all you can between now and then. Can you do that?"

Zac nodded vigorously.

"Second, stay out of trouble. I mean it. No drugs, no police. If you ever go to jail, you can forget about becoming a soldier. Understand?"

"Yes, sir."

"All right then. You come back here when you're eighteen, and we'll talk again, okay?"

They shook hands. Before we left, the man gave Zac a handful of "Be all that you can be" posters and brochures. He carried them out like they were medals.

We drove most of the way home in silence. At first, Zac was content just looking at his posters and trying to read the brochures. But he kept coming back to one particular brochure. Its cover showed a young soldier in brown face paint, standing tall under a cloudless blue sky—gun at the ready and eyes locked on a distant hill. He looked strong, courageous, and ready to meet his destiny.

After a bit, Zac sighed. "How come it takes so long to grow up?"

"Oh, it just seems like it takes a long time. You'll be grown up before you know it," I said.

"I don't want to wait, Mom. I want to be a soldier right now."

"But think, Zac. If you were a soldier right now, you couldn't carry very much. Your arms aren't nearly as strong as they'll be when you're eighteen. The other soldiers would probably have to carry your stuff for you."

"I'm going to be stronger than Dad when I'm eighteen."

"Well, Dad's pretty strong…but I'm sure you'll pass him up." I smiled.

"What else?" Zac asked.

I thought for a second. "You'll be taller."

"What's that good for?"

"You want to drive the tank, don't you?"

He grinned. "Well, yeah."

"They'd never let you drive right now. You couldn't see out the…uh…tank window thing." I was rapidly running out of soldier information.

Zac was quiet for a minute, staring out the window. "I

wish I could grow all at once. I wish I could make my bones grow right now."

"They'll grow," I assured him. "They're growing even as we speak. Just be patient."

We pulled into the parking space in front of our apartment. Johnny was sitting on the grass near our walkway, waiting for Zac to get out of the car.

"Thanks, Mom." He slammed the door and ran across the lawn to share his news and show off his bounty. He gestured wildly as he dropped his goodies on the ground and unrolled one of his posters. I couldn't hear him, but I could see he was giving Johnny an earful.

My heart swelled as I watched him. He'd polished his boots on the drive to the recruiting center, using shoe polish he borrowed from his dad. The toes gleamed in the sunlight. His fingers fought to poke themselves out of sleeves that were much too long. His helmet slipped and slid all over his little head.

He was a little boy, standing there in full army gear, wanting desperately to be a man. "Oh, Lord," I breathed. "Please take Your time turning my baby into a soldier."

I loved him so much it hurt, and I wished I could convince him that it would all work out perfectly in its own time. I wished I could ease his restlessness and calm his longings and help him love every day between now and his dreams.

He was just my baby. That's all he was. My baby in an army suit, all dressed up with no place to go. It would take years for those little arms to fill those big sleeves. And I was okay with that.

Then, as I sat there in the warmth of my car, smiling and loving my son, I heard the Lord whisper.

You've got little arms, too.

He opened my eyes and showed me a picture of myself, standing there in Zac's place—a little girl in a suit with sleeves much too long for my arms. Chomping at the bit.

Certain I'm ready for the battle. Wishing I could be wiser and more mature, and longing for the time when I would have a fit and ready word for every occasion. Wanting tomorrow things today.

"Do You really think these arms are little, Father?"

Yes, they're little—but they're just right for now.

And they're growing every day.